A DICTIONARY OF EMOTIONS IN A TIME OF WAR
20 SHORT WORKS BY UKRAINIAN PLAYWRIGHTS

Pavlo Arie, Olena Astaseva, Ihor Bilyts, Natalia Blok, Andriy Bondarenko, Vitaliy Chenskiy, Julia Gonchar, Oksana Grytsenko, Olena Hapieieva, Iryna Harets, Anastasiia Kosodii, Maksym Kurochkin, Tetiana Kytsenko, Lena Lagushonkova, Olha Maciupa, Yevhen Markovskiy, Kateryna Penkova, Oksana Savchenko, Liudmyla Tymoshenko, and Natalka Vorozhbyt

Translated by John Freedman, Natalia Bratus, John Farndon, and Evgenia Kovryga

Compiled, edited, and introduced by John Freedman

Egret
Chapel Hill, 2023

A DICTIONARY OF EMOTIONS IN A TIME OF WAR

The Texts of Kyiv's Theater of Playwrights: Literary-Based Acts of War, copyright © 2022 by John Freedman | *A Dictionary of Emotions in a Time of War,* copyright © 2022 by Olena Astaseva, translation copyright © 2022 by John Freedman | *Call Things by Their Names,* copyright © 2022 by Tetiana Kytsenko, translation copyright © 2022 by John Freedman and Natalia Bratus | *The Peed-Upon Armored Personnel Carrier,* copyright © 2022 by Oksana Grytsenko, translation copyright © 2022 by John Freedman and Natalia Bratus | *How to Talk to the Dead,* copyright © 2022 by Anastasiia Kosodii, translation copyright © 2022 by John Freedman and Natalia Bratus | *Survivor's Syndrome,* copyright © 2022 by Andriy Bondarenko, translation copyright © 2022 by John Freedman and Natalia Bratus | *A Topol-M Rocket Fired at a Cat Named Brooch,* copyright © 2022 by Lena Lagushonkova, translation copyright © 2022 by John Freedman and Natalia Bratus | *A Sense of War,* copyright © 2022 by Julia Gonchar, translation copyright © 2022 by John Farndon and Evgenia Kovryga | *Robinson,* copyright © 2022 by Vitaliy Chenskiy, translation copyright © 2022 by John Freedman | *Our Children,* copyright © 2022 by Natalia Blok, translation copyright © 2022 by John Freedman and Natalia Bratus | *TDP [Temporarily Displaced Persons]* copyright © 2022 by Kateryna Penkova, translation copyright © 2022 by John Freedman and Natalia Bratus | *My Tara,* copyright © 2022 by Liudmyla Tymoshenko, translation copyright © 2022 by John Freedman and Natalia Bratus | *I Want to Go Home,* copyright © 2022 by Oksana Savchenko, translation copyright © 2022 by John Freedman and Natalia Bratus | *Diary of Survival of a Civilian Urbanite in Conditions of War,* copyright © 2022 by Pavlo Arie, translation copyright © 2022 by John Freedman and Natalia Bratus | *In the Bowels of the Earth,* copyright © 2022 by Olena Hapieieva, translation copyright © 2022 by John Freedman and Natalia Bratus | *Planting an Apple Tree,* copyright © 2022 by Iryna Harets, translation copyright © 2022 by John Freedman and Natalia Bratus | *Flowering,* copyright © 2022 by Olha Maciupa, translation copyright © 2022 by John Farndon | *The Russian Soldier,* copyright © 2022 by Ihor Bilyts, translation copyright © 2022 by John Freedman | *Three Rendezvous,* copyright © 2022 by Natalka Vorozhbyt, translation copyright © 2022 by John Freedman and Natalia Bratus | *Eight Songs,* copyright © 2022 by Yevhen Markovskiy, translation copyright © 2023 by John Freedman | *Three Attempts to Improve Daily Life,* copyright © 2022 by Maksym Kurochkin, translation copyright © 2022 by John Freedman and Natalia Bratus | anthology copyright © 2023 by Laertes Press

Cover and book design by Maxine Mills
ALL RIGHTS RESERVED
Printed in the United States of America
Second Edition
Library of Congress Control Number: 2023935488
ISBN: 978-1-942281-44-3

First published as an acting edition in January, 2023 (ISBN: 978-1-942281-33-7), this edition is a reformatting that includes a selection by Yevhen Markovskiy (missing from the first edition) and updates to the introduction.

CONTENTS

The Texts of Kyiv's Theater of Playwrights:
Literary-Based Acts of War — *John Freedman*   5

A Dictionary of Emotions in a Time of War
— *Olena Astaseva*   41

Call Things by Their Names — *Tetiana Kytsenko*   67

The Peed-Upon Armored Personnel Carrier
— *Oksana Grytsenko*   73

How to Talk to the Dead — *Anastasiia Kosodii*   77

Survivor's Syndrome — *Andriy Bondarenko*   81

A Topol-M Rocket Fired at a Cat Named Brooch
— *Lena Lagushonkova*   107

A Sense of War — *Julia Gonchar*   117

Robinson — *Vitaliy Chenskiy*   127

Our Children — *Natalia Blok*   141

TDP [Temporarily Displaced Persons]
— *Kateryna Penkova* — 151

My Tara — *Liudmyla Tymoshenko* — 155

I Want to Go Home — *Oksana Savchenko* — 161

Diary of Survival of a Civilian Urbanite in Conditions of War — *Pavlo Arie* — 171

In the Bowels of the Earth — *Olena Hapieieva* — 213

Planting an Apple Tree — *Iryna Harets* — 231

Flowering — *Olha Maciupa* — 239

The Russian Soldier — *Ihor Bilyts* — 249

Three Rendezvous — *Natalka Vorozhbyt* — 255

Eight Songs — *Yevhen Markovskiy* — 267

Three Attempts to Improve Daily Life — *Maksym Kurochkin* — 279

Biographies — 285

THE TEXTS OF KYIV'S THEATER OF PLAYWRIGHTS: LITERARY-BASED ACTS OF WAR

BY JOHN FREEDMAN

THE BACKSTORY

Nobody knew in the second half of February 2022 that any of these texts would ever appear in the world. A whole different set was being written.

Twenty writers working under the banner of the not-quite-yet-existing Theater of Playwrights had scheduled their venue's grand opening for March 12. Artistic Director Maksym Kurochkin was getting the group's renovated semi-basement in Kyiv prepared to receive spectators and helping to evaluate a stack of short texts being submitted by his colleagues to be read as part of the theater's inaugural festivities. It was to be a memorable night, the birth of a promising cultural institution in a city that, despite the paradoxically debilitating, albeit largely successful, Maidan Revolution in 2013/2014, and eight ensuing years of smoldering, deadly war less than 500 miles to the east of Ukraine's capital, was in the process of experiencing a cultural boom.

The internationally celebrated Kurochkin, along with the equally renowned playwright, screenwriter, and director Natalka Vorozhbyt, had seen a large number of talented, independent-minded, unique, and variously accomplished writers converge around them. Each writer, within the framework of this more or less collectively conceived theater, was poised to begin making their individual mark on Ukrainian drama.

These plans were dashed when, at approximately 5 a.m. on 24 February 2022, the Russian army mounted a massive invasion of Ukraine. A long, 40-mile column of Russian tanks headed for Kyiv in the west, while an amphibious assault was mounted on Mariupol in the south, and Russian bombs and rockets pounded targets in Kharkiv and Chernihiv in the north, Dnipro in the center of the country, Odesa in the southwest, and elsewhere. Russian president Vladimir Putin called the invasion a "special military operation," and the Russian government almost immediately began handing out prison terms to Russians who dared publicly to refer to what was happening as "war."

My purpose, however, is not to tell the story of Russia's war against Ukraine. That is done beautifully, in deeply personal vignettes, with wit, insight, horror, emotion, and poetry in the texts collected in this book. My task is to describe how these unique monologues and dialogues came into being, and to provide some information to fill out the picture inside, outside, and around the texts.

Pardon some of the personal viewpoints that follow, but there is no other way for me to tell this story.

I can only begin by noting a message I received from William Wong, a director, actor, and teacher in Hong Kong. William had taken part frequently in the

Insulted. Belarus Worldwide Reading Project, a long-running program I was curating to publicize the horrible reality of the courageous, but ultimately unsuccessful, revolution in Minsk, Belarus, in the fall of 2020. No sooner had the Russian invasion of Ukraine begun than William sent me the following query: "Can we do a worldwide reading of a Ukrainian play to support them?"

My first reaction was, "Indeed, can we?!" and I immediately reached out to colleagues who I thought might help. They included Molly Flynn, an American scholar based in London, the English writer and translator John Farndon, and two of the best Ukrainian playwrights alive — Natalka Vorozhbyt and Maksym Kurochkin. Molly sent play translations, emails, and advice; John responded he would help me take on translations immediately; Natalka sent English translations of two of her plays and encouraged me to contact Maksym, because he was the artistic director of a new playwrights' theater in Kyiv, and he should have access to a large number of brand new texts.

The information about Maksym's new theater was, indeed, news to me. I immediately reached out to him and explained I was mounting a project that even I, at that moment, did not yet know would end up being called the Worldwide Ukrainian Play Readings. I naively assumed my 25-year working friendship with Maksym would be more than enough justification for him to send me everything I asked for. But, plead as I might that I needed texts as quickly as possible, Maksym refused to send anything that had been written for the planned March opening. On 7 March, even as the first readings of other texts were already taking shape in Hong Kong, the U.S., Finland, Germany, Slovakia, and elsewhere, he wrote: "I think it would be wrong to give out those short plays. They already belong to another, prewar era . . . I think it would be logical for the theaters of the world to commission from Ukrainian playwrights hastily written plays about the day-to-day situation. [...] I would be happy to lobby this project among the playwrights of the Theater of Playwrights. But this way we will retain control of the discourse. That is important" (Kurochkin).

So there it is, the germination of the book you hold in your hands. Now the plan had to be put into action.

For that I turned to two old friends and colleagues, Philip Arnoult of the Center for International Theatre Development (CITD) in Baltimore, MD, and Noah Birksted-Breen, the founder of Sputnik Theatre in London. Noah answered immediately, writing that he wanted very much to be a part of the project, and that, difficult financial times be damned, he was willing to empty his theater's coffers in order to commission a play from one writer. Philip, whose organization has been supporting theater in the U.S., Eastern and Central Europe, the Netherlands, and Africa for over four decades, also shot back an instantaneous positive reply. CITD committed to funding the writing of 15 texts, later following up with several more commissions and grants for the Theater of Playwrights.

Maksym determined the size of the grants when I asked if $500 per short text would be sufficient. "$500 is good money for good times," he replied. "$1000 for a short play, now that would be support." And so it was — the preliminaries were done and, before long, brand new texts began flowing into my inbox as grant money was traveling the wires from the U.S. and U.K. to Ukraine.

THE CONTEXT

One could say the impulse bringing these texts into existence had been felt by Ukrainians for ages. And by that I mean centuries. There is no proper way to understand Ukrainian writers today without understanding the journey their culture has taken.

The origins of Kyiv, and, therefore, Kyivan Rus, officially go back to the eighth or ninth centuries, depending upon your source and point of view. Quite understandably, Ukraine claims the hallowed grounds of Kyiv on the banks of the mighty Dnipro River as its own. Russia, however, whose name is derived from the ancient civilization of "Rus," began exerting its own claim on this land as its own spiritual and historical origin around the 16th century. For most of the second millennium, Kyiv found itself in a position of subservience to the Mongolian Golden Horde, the Grand Duchy of Lithuania, the Kingdom of Poland, the Russian empire, and then the Soviet empire.

It is of no small interest that an anthology of Ukrainian literature published in 1921 by the renowned French linguist Antoine Meillet dated what he called the "first renaissance" of Ukrainian letters precisely to the late 16th century. The "second renaissance" he placed in the early 19th century, leading to a period of "great masters" in the middle of that century (Meillet).

That said, we can look to 1798 as a turning point for Ukrainian culture in general, and Ukrainian literature in specific. Although ballads, tales, poetry, historical and religious texts had existed in the oral or manuscript traditions for some time, 1798 saw the first-ever publication of a Ukrainian-language poem, Ivan Kotliarevsky's *Eneida,* a parody of Virgil's *Aeneid* set in the Zaporizhzhia region. That same year also saw the first publication of works, in St. Petersburg, of the famed philosopher Hryhorii Skovoroda. Whether he was writing poetry, prose, history, or philosophy, Skovoroda employed a unique mix of Old Church Slavonic, Ukrainian vernacular, Russian, Latin, and Greek. The first published Ukrainian-language novel, *Marusia* by Hryhorii Kvitka-Osnovianenko, followed 36 years later.

By the 1840s a flourishing of national literature was underway, led by the poet Taras Shevchenko, a former serf who was freed in 1838, and whose works, especially the 1845 epistle, "To my Living, Dead, and Still Unborn Countrymen, Both in Ukraine and Beyond," galvanized in the minds of those countrymen the notion that Ukraine was a separate, self-sufficient nation. Russian authorities arrested Shevchenko two years later and sent him into exile, banning him from writing for a decade, a draconian act that only enhanced his reputation as a national poet, prophet, and martyr.

While fellow Ukrainian Nikolai Gogol chose to write in Russian and focus primarily on comic aspects of Ukrainian and Russian life, Shevchenko powerfully focused his poetic attention "on Ukraine, her experiences, especially her trauma, her subjugation and destruction in the past and especially in the present. In itself, of course, this was a profoundly revolutionary act: his Ukrainian readers, and especially his contemporaries — the first to be exposed to his poetry — were not only aware of this but overwhelmed by it" (Grabowicz).

Words of similar sentiment may someday be written about the texts contained in this collection. And it is important to pause amidst this brief historical discussion to point out the connections between the writers of the Theater of

Playwrights and their predecessors. Virtually every one of the works published here takes on, to one degree or another, the trauma, attempted subjugation, and attempted destruction of contemporary Ukraine by Russia. Moreover, every single one of them is intended, if not as a profoundly revolutionary act, then surely as a profound, literary-based act of war.

In *A Dictionary of Emotions in a Time of War,* Olena Astaseva writes, "When you hear the sound of a shell flying at your house, at first you feel fear, then hatred. Hatred for whoever did it. For all of Russia, for all its inhabitants without exception."

In *Our Children,* Natalia Blok writes about a friend who said he had "been waiting for war a long time, and that Ukraine would win, that Russia had signed its own death warrant, and would fall apart in a few years . . ."

In *I Want to Go Home,* Oksana Savchenko writes, "The Russians captured the stables and starved the horses. Starved them. One man tried to reach the horses to feed them, but he was killed by the Russian beasts. Killed. Russian whores kill people. Does it make sense to talk about starving horses when Russian Orcs are killing civilians in Ukraine?"

Writing in the *New York Times*, Jason Farago pointed directly to what I designate as a literary-based act of war: "With Russia actively trying to erase Ukraine's national identity," he writes, "this country's music, literature, movies and monuments are not recreations. They are battlefields" (Farago).

Oleksii Makarenko, founder of the online Gasoline Radio station in Kyiv, also stresses the notion that the war with Russia is not merely geopolitical, it is cultural. Speaking specifically of indigenous, Ukrainian music, he told a reporter for *The Guardian*, "If you learn the music, the folklore, you will see the difference between us and Russia. In that way, it is a real weapon" (Mulhall).

The texts in this collection are filled not only with a scathing hatred for the geographical neighbor to the east, but also a deep affection for Ukrainians and things Ukrainian. In many of these texts we see an effort to define the national character, to set it in sharp contrast against the Russian ways that have been enforced upon Ukrainians for centuries.

In *Call Things by Their Names,* Tetiana Kytsenko writes, "But here's what I think: even if a Russian understands the language, will they really understand Ukrainians? It's not even a matter of the meaning of the words, but what stands behind them. Take, for example, our leading national virtue — 'sincerity.' It's not just a matter of being 'frank.' It is an odd fusion of cordiality and breadth of soul mixed with frank honesty — the ability to call things by their proper names."

In his short poem "Testament," Shevchenko wrote:

… Bury me then stand,
Break your shackles
And shower your freedom
With the enemy's evil blood …

The only difference I might expect had this poem been written by one of the 20 authors collected here, would be, "Bury *the enemy* then stand …"

There is no timidity in the writers collected here, no sense of trepidation before a powerful geopolitical neighbor that, for the last 500 years or so, has rarely hesitated to suppress and repress the smaller nation on its western border. The

Russian aggression of 2022 unleashed a nearly unbounded fury in Ukrainians. Hundreds of years of Ukrainians seeking more or less quietly, unobtrusively, and diplomatically to find common ground with the dominant Russian culture hit the equivalent of a brick wall when the Russian military breached the Ukrainian border. Another way to picture it would be as a long-neglected abscess that burst with explosive force. The response was instant and fierce. Everything Russian became anathema. It didn't matter who or what it was — whether it was a street named after a Russian artist, a monument honoring a Russian poet (even if his name was Alexander Pushkin), or just some shared cultural reference to a universally known literary work.

Ukrainian frustration about Russian dominance in all things increased constantly after the nation declared independence on 24 August 1991. Scholarly and popular conversations about whether Mikhail Bulgakov, of *The Master and Margarita* fame, was a Russian or Ukrainian writer were underway a full five years before Maidan began, and nearly 16 years before the Russian invasion. "It's a cultural cold war with little sign of tensions easing," wrote an author in *The Guardian* (Nestruck).

But forget Bulgakov, Gogol, or even Anton Chekhov (who wrote several of his most important plays while living in Yalta on the Crimean Peninsula). Arguments about the soup named borscht became heated. Was it a Ukrainian or Russian national dish? New York–based Ukrainian chef Olesia Lew told a BBC reporter, "Yes, Russian people claim it's their food. But it's a food they developed through occupation" (Evans).

No longer were the inhabitants of Ukraine willing to define any part of their life and traditions by way of anything Russian. Some Russians and westerners decried what they perceived to be "cancel culture," as Ukrainians figuratively and actively purged mentions, hints, or allusions to Russian culture in all aspects of life, from the official to the personal. *"How can you possibly deny the importance of Pushkin, Tolstoy, and Dostoevsky?"* these observers asked incredulously. What such viewpoints failed to take into account, however, was that, in essence, Ukrainian society and culture were not attempting to erase or destroy anything; theirs was a much more subtle and more creative act. They wanted, finally, after hundreds of years of seeing their own culture forced into a subservient role, to fill the places of public honor with individuals who spoke like them, thought like them, and shared common values and aspirations.

Vitaliy Chenskiy alludes briefly to this cultural battle in *Robinson,* where his narrator describes preparing to read his "beloved Dostoevsky" by candlelight, but later adds purposefully not taking his Dostoevsky novel out on the street ("God forbid!") where patrolmen might check his possessions and have reason to question his loyalties. The "God forbid!" exclamation is a knowing one, a light-hearted wink, an admission of a paradox that has entered his life but does not define it. For Chenskiy, at least, this is an opportunity to inject some humor into his tale, not much more.

Historically, however, the problem was far from funny most of the time.

The influence of Shevchenko encouraged the appearance in the mid-19th century of numerous noteworthy writers, including Mikola Kostomarov, Panteliemon Kulish, and Maria Markovich (pseudonym Marko Vovchok). They stood poised to establish the language and literature of Ukraine as worthy contributors to world culture. The Russian authorities, however, like their subsequent Soviet counterparts, were unwilling to tolerate that. Time and again Ukrainian writers were subjugated to repressions that were intended to keep them as invisible as possible, if not to destroy them outright. Lesia Ukrainka, a poet and playwright now recognized as one of the greatest of all Ukrainian writers, could not publish her first collection of poems within the Russian empire. It had to be printed in 1893 in the city we now know as Lviv, then called Lemberg, in the eastern part of the Austro-Hungarian empire, and smuggled across the border.

"In the early 19th century, Russian publishers accepted Ukrainian literature only if it was ethnographic, comedic, or apolitical. (Serious literature had to be in Russian.) Successive laws in 1863 and 1876 led to the effective banning of all works in the Ukrainian language, as well as their near-complete prohibition in public settings. In the 1930s, Stalin executed a whole generation of writers who had been rebuilding Ukrainian literary culture in the decade prior, brutally cutting short the growth of the country's vibrant avant-garde" (Blacker).

Indeed, Stalin's brutality toward Ukraine was extreme even for this tyrant. After his policies brought about the Holodomor, an orchestrated famine that killed four to five million Ukrainians in 1932 and 1933, he turned his attention over the next seven years to the sphere of the arts, literally wiping out an entire generation of writers who were on the verge of bringing Ukrainian literature to new heights. In what subsequently became known as the Executed Renaissance, no fewer than 223 Ukrainian writers were imprisoned, exiled, or murdered.

". . . A painful mark of twentieth century Ukrainian history; its tragic peak [was] the mass execution of nearly three hundred members of the Ukrainian renaissance at Sandarmokh, a mass killing site in Karelia, northwest Russia. Some estimates assert that nearly 30,000 Ukrainian intellectuals were repressed during the Stalinist Yezhovschina, and its impact on literary contributions can be seen in the change in publication trends of that decade. While in 1930, the works of 259 Ukrainian writers were published, by 1938 only 36 of those writers remained — the rest were executed, exiled, had disappeared, or committed suicide" (Perehinets).

One hears in the calls to de-Russianize Ukrainian culture a pained appeal to recover the names of writers, thinkers, artists, and musicians whose works have been shuffled aside by history and, more importantly, politics. Why, indeed, should a young Ukrainian girl live on, say, Pushkin Street, while she is denied access to useful knowledge, or even basic information, about hundreds of local, homegrown talents, many of whom might be able to exert life-changing influence on her? For those in the know — and this, significantly, has been lost on virtually everyone outside of Ukraine for hundreds of years — Ukrainian literature has been not only "an autonomous aesthetic system," but also "an instrument for political struggle mostly devoted to the (re)awakening of a Ukrainian national consciousness and the subsequent regaining of national independence..." (Achilli).

The texts comprising this collection, along with other, subsequent works written by these and other contemporary Ukrainian writers, will eventually be seen and evaluated in the context of the contemporary reawakening of Ukrainian national consciousness.

This is made especially true by a handful of statements and one long essay attributed to Russian president Vladimir Putin in the run-up to his invasion of Ukraine. Putin in 2021 amused some, astonished many, and angered many more, when he uncharacteristically assumed the role of a philosopher-head of state, and published a pseudo-scholarly analysis of Ukrainian and Russian history whose purpose, essentially, was to deprive Ukraine of any claims to possessing an indigenous culture separate from Russia's. In his essay, "On the Historical Unity of Russians and Ukrainians," Putin frequently employed the offensive, long-abandoned reference to Ukraine and Ukrainians as "Little Russia," or "Malorussians," declaring that the notion of an independent Ukraine was bogus, and was foisted on the world, historically, by Poland and, more recently, the West. "The idea of Ukrainian people as a nation separate from the Russians started to form and gain ground among the Polish elite and a part of the Malorussian intelligentsia," Putin wrote.

"Since there was no historical basis — and could not have been any —" Putin, or a ghost writer, continued, "conclusions were substantiated by all sorts of concoctions, which went as far as to claim that the Ukrainians are the true Slavs and the Russians, the Muscovites, are not. Such 'hypotheses' became increasingly used for political purposes as a tool of rivalry between European states" (On the Historical Unity).

Putin expanded upon these thoughts at an extraordinary, protracted press conference in the wee hours of the morning of 24 February 2022, immediately before sending his army into Ukraine. Those of us who heard it detected in it a shrill note of hysteria. Others, like Julia Gonchar, who references Putin's comments in this collection in *A Sense of War,* are more sanguine about it, letting their anger explode in response to other topics and incidents. In any case, even as most Ukrainians were still in bed sleeping, and Russian tanks were already rolling through the Belarus countryside toward Kyiv, Putin continued to push his inane theory that Ukraine didn't exist. The texts in this collection exist to assert precisely the opposite.

THE TEXTS

The texts herein are written in various genres — documentary style, poetry, prose, social media posts, telephone texting, historical tales, memoirs, monologues, and dramatic dialogues. Most were written in March 2022, although two were written in late June. One was completed in November, and a group of songs by Yevhen Markovskiy did not surface until February 2023. All share one thing in common — to one extent or another they are confessional. They are raw, even when, as in the case of Pavlo Arie's *Diary of Survival of a Civilian Urbanite in Conditions of War,* their author makes a concerted effort to avoid the mindset and language of panic and anger.

The choice of language is usually Ukrainian. In the years following the Maidan uprising, Ukrainian was embraced enthusiastically and wholeheartedly by most inhabitants of Ukraine, regardless of nationality, and by virtually all people of culture. To speak Ukrainian in Ukraine, Europe, or anywhere else today is to make a statement. It is a badge of pride and honor, an opportunity to declare one's loyalties. It is an expression of a deep emotional tie to the land of one's birth. Ukrainian president Volodymyr Zelenskiy began his time in office speaking primarily in Russian, in part because his Ukrainian was noticeably weak. That changed quickly once the war began. Very soon thereafter he would resort to the language of the enemy only when seeking to reach out to, and communicate directly with, the populace of Russia. Dual-language individuals who, in the past, would surely have switched to Russian out of courtesy, ease, or need depending upon the capabilities of their interlocutor, now might not make that shift. They may seek a third language to share if Ukrainian isn't accessible to all.

Writers like Kurochkin and Vorozhbyt, who gained international fame as "Russian" or "Russian-language" playwrights, now work exclusively in Ukrainian. Vorozhbyt has famously said time and again that "letters are not to blame" for the crimes that Russia has committed against Ukraine. Yet I hardly know a Ukrainian writer who has not bristled, at least internally, when confronted with the need to express themselves in Russian.

The battle of language and expression is both the theme and the territory of Tetiana Kytsenko's *Call Things by Their Names*. Significantly, she identifies her work as a "war-ning," a cautionary tale about the dangers of language, words, labels, and names. "Of course," Kytsenko writes, "everyone in Ukraine will understand Russian. But will a Russian understand anything here?"

"By the way," she concludes, "about names: I've noticed one interesting nuance. It's not so recognizable in everyday life, because I speak both Ukrainian and Russian. But when corresponding in English, I have noticed feeling irritation when foreign colleagues address me not as Tetiana, but rather by using the Russian version. My dear friends, Tatiana is something else entirely. The difference of one letter is enough to contain an entire worldview."

Of the twenty texts in this collection only five employ Russian in part or whole. But only one of those authors, Vitaliy Chenskiy in *Robinson*, seems to have made his choice rather casually. In *A Dictionary of Emotions in a Time of War, Parts I and II*, Olena Astaseva occasionally addresses Russian-speaking friends directly or indirectly, and her choice, like that of President Zelenskiy after the advent of the war, is most likely dictated by her desire to communicate her pained thoughts to those Russians who refuse to believe there is a war going on, or that the Russian army has engaged in any aggressive or murderous acts.

In "Slovianochka-Kubanochka," one of his *Eight Songs*, Yevhen Markovskiy allows a Ukrainian lyric to morph into Russian, signaling the moment of transition when his hometown of Kherson was occupied by the enemy.

Ihor Bilyts made a unique linguistic choice in his short piece entitled *The Russian Soldier*. As if an ironic response to Vorozhbyt's claim that "letters are not to blame," he writes the entire piece in Russian words, but spells them using Ukrainian letters. Most likely this is merely a nod to realism since all the characters are Russians in Russia, and they, of course, would speak only Russian. But by using the Ukrainian alphabet to spell the words they speak, Bilyts not only puts distance between the characters, himself, and, presumably, the reader, but he actually, to an extent, "destroys" the Russian he uses. It looks silly, it looks foreign, and it looks helpless dressed in those Ukrainian letters. Such nuances are lost in translation, of course, but it is significant and interesting to know what is taking place on micro-levels.

Finally among the five that employ Russian to certain degrees, there is Olena Hapieieva's *In the Bowels of the Earth*, a linguistically, structurally and narratively chaotic piece. The chaos, naturally, is an authorial choice. In this, one of the longer pieces of the collection, Hapieieva observes a large number of adults, children, family members, and strangers in a basement bomb shelter during an air raid. They are thrown together unnaturally and temporarily, but with significant consequences, at least in the short term. They have no choice but to deal with neighbors sitting or lying foot-to-shoulder with them, people they most likely would not choose to spend time with under normal circumstances. Some of them speak Russian, most speak Ukrainian, while the switching back and forth between languages tends to be jarring and unsettling.

One cannot help but feel suspicions arise when Russian is introduced into the narrative. Again, there is no way to approximate in English the full effect of the linguistic play, and so, as translator, I added a few stage directions to let anyone encountering the text know that it contains shifts in dynamics.

Hapieieva also plays visually with a kind of poetic structure by centering all of the lines on the page. This is no haphazard choice on her part; I have translated other of her works that are written in the same way. It is clearly a part of her aesthetic vision. And, although most of the work is written with the usual character identifications at the beginning of each line, Hapieieva will occasionally drop the identifiers and leave several consecutive lines of free-standing speech, the nameless and faceless voices that also inhabit this cramped, noisy, claustrophobic territory.

In *Flowering*, Olha Maciupa incorporates two poems into a free-flowing narrative that wanders carefully among memory, dream, history, and biography. There is, hiding behind her resilience, a sense of doom and helplessness. "Trees are blooming," she writes. "Cherries, apricots, apple trees. Magnolias are blooming and for the first time in my life I can't enjoy flowering. My time has stopped."

Other authors, like Andriy Bondarenko in *Survivor's Syndrome*, and Anastasiia Kosodii in *How to Talk to the Dead,* do more than merely hint at poetic structures; they place their texts firmly in a poetic framework.

Bondarenko unleashes a long whiplash assault of words in this, the second-longest of these texts, chasing words and meanings up one side of his consciousness and down the other.

What kind of world is this?
This is a world of war. And
what is war?
It is something that cannot
be. Ever. But it is. How can
that be? It cannot be. We live
in a world that cannot be.
What could not happen has
happened. The unspeakable
has happened, the unreal
has happened.
Are we alive at all,
we who survived?

War begets denial and repudiation at every turn. Life is not life. Reality is not real.

Where are we? Our places
and spaces have been
replaced, spread out,
confused. Train stations
function, but they are no
longer train stations. Cafés
function, but they're not
cafés. People sit and drink,
but that is no longer drinking.

Everything in a time of war is a negation of itself. The text begins at "The End" and works and wanders its way back to "The Beginning." But in neither place (for "all places have been replaced") will the narrator ever recognize himself again. Never again shall the twain of personality meet. Bondarenko here is not interested in the pain he may feel, or the insults and humiliations he may have been subjected to. As one would expect in a poetic work, he takes a stance above the fray of the world he observes and seeks to make sense of the irreconcilable paradoxes that have invaded every aspect of his waking and thinking life. Or, as he puts it in reference to deciphering what the future may be like, "We must learn this from / zero, from scratch, from the / emptiness of the day's / eternal gloom."

Aside from Part II of Astaseva's *A Dictionary of Emotions*, which was added in June 2022, Kosodii's *How to Talk to the Dead* is one of just four texts written when the war was no longer new (the others being Kateryna Penkova's *TDP [Temporarily Displaced Persons]*, Maksym Kurochkin's *Three Attempts to Improve Daily Life,* and Yevhen Markovskiy's *Eight Songs)*. One senses that in the opening segment, a kind of world-weary journalistic observation that blankly describes witnessed atrocities. There is none of the shock and surprise expressed in texts written in the early days of the war, none of the hurt of being misunderstood or misconstrued. These are words written long after the murderous blow of the massacres in Bucha, Irpin, or Mariupol had come and gone from the world's newscasts. They are words full of a heavy, impenetrable, unwanted knowledge of life. One short paragraph describing a memory brings forth the stunning, unforgettable phrase that a quoted character utters about the dead: "They died so badly. I, at least, will talk to them."

Inspired by this utterance from a man who has taken to digging up dead, discarded bodies, Kosodii's narrator slips into a reverie of real or imagined snippets of memory. It doesn't matter to whom the images belong — the dead or the living — they are still ways of reclaiming lost life. The brief, hard-hitting piece concludes with some stray thoughts about, and strategies for, the future, perhaps landing not far from territory tilled by Bondarenko in *Survivor's Syndrome:* "There will be," Kosodii writes, "such words as have never been."

How to Talk to the Dead was written specifically for a triumphant evening of readings held 24 June 2022 at the future home of the Theater of Playwrights, a semi-basement hall in the historical Podil neighborhood of Kyiv. Maksym Kurochkin, like most of his countrymen aged 18 to 60, had laid aside his laptop and had taken up the tools of war to defend his native land. He was wounded in early June and sent home to Kyiv for three weeks of rest and recovery. Literally one night before heading back to active service, he gathered a full house of colleagues and friends to hear writers and performers deliver texts written in the previous days and hours. Kurochkin declined to call this the theater's opening event, insisting instead that it was merely an opportunity to mark the beginning of the fifth month of war.

Also penned specifically for that late June evening was Penkova's *TDP*. Here we sense the numbing effect the war has had on the narrator, someone, most likely, quite similar to Penkova, who helps refugees find temporary places to stay. Tragedy is left far beyond the edge of the page. Nobody wastes time or breath on complaints or tears. A man from the godforsaken hellhole that once was the city of Mariupol only states his son needs to give a DNA sample as they search for his missing mother. What could possibly have caused a mother in

Mariupol to have gone missing? Another needs a first-floor room because he is on crutches. A family of four with three cats and a Chihuahua is simply making a "hasty departure." The horror of the tragic details behind each of these vignettes is obvious to anyone in the know. Those who know it like Penkova don't need to spell it out.

Following a reading of several of these texts by the Shipley Players in West Yorkshire, U.K., director Ged Quayle wrote, "That was amazing. That was truly genuinely amazing. Laughs were heard, despite the themes. Tears were shed" (Quayle). The comment about tears needs no justification. It is the reference to laughter that, perhaps requires some attention, for, indeed, humor is a frequent companion in most of the pieces, no matter how implacable they may be.

Natalka Vorozhbyt, whose dark, hard-hitting film *Bad Roads* was the Ukrainian nominee for the 2022 Academy Awards, is famed for her sardonic, sometimes challenging humor. That is evident in the three segments of her *Three Rendezvous,* written expressly for this collection. But don't expect Vorozhbyt ever to make you laugh without making you cringe at the same time. The first segment shows us a clumsily humorous attempt at online sex between two lovers separated by war, but the ending appears to be anything but funny. The second presents a café-based conversation between two men in Kyiv, one of whom still worries about the behavior of his former wife, who escaped to Munich. The brief final vignette, basically written as a screenplay, leaves a curious Austrian man shaken out of his romantic reveries when he sees the lengths a mysterious Ukrainian woman will go to dishonor a monument to a Russian soldier.

Lena Lagushonkova's humor in *A Topol-M Rocket Fired at a Cat Named Brooch* is somewhere to the lighter side of Vorozhbyt's, but still tends to be several shades of black. "The rats here don't howl," she writes, "they're local." Or, "A rocket lands in the neighboring yard. It did not land there on purpose, it was shot down. But it's unpleasant all the same."

Perhaps the most iconic moment in Lagushonkova's text is her claim, "I do not want Russian cats to suffer." No matter what evil fate she might wish upon the invaders, that does not apply to their furry domestic friends.

Animals in general, and cats in specific, are frequent visitors in many of the texts in this collection. You will remember the displaced family in Penkova's *Temporarily Displaced Persons* who are transporting three cats and a dog. Animals are, in hellish moments, a connection to warmth, comfort, and affection. I think it is proper, and even necessary, to reveal that Natalia Bratus, a co-translator on 15 of the Ukrainian-language texts published here, arrived in my town as a refugee from Ukraine with her daughter, grandson, a large, inscrutable and magisterial cat named Basia, and a splendid, high-strung German shepherd named Kora. The five of them make a cohesive family unit, and there is something very Ukrainian in that, something I see cropping up in many of the texts here. A large part of *Topol-M* revolves around a social media discussion involving numerous people in various countries trying to help save a cat that was abandoned by its family in the city of Hostomel in the early days of the war.

Oksana Grytsenko's *The Peed-upon Armored Personnel Carrier* strikes me as an example of national humor that could mark her as a descendant of Nikolai Gogol, at least in his early career. *Personnel Carrier* is virtually a classical, narrative short story. Its details are marvelous and often unexpected. Its characters, though none stand out alone, are portrayed vividly, usually by just a few words or actions, including the one mentioned in the title. There is a loving irony to this tale that suggests if the author wanted to write a wicked satire taking these people and their village down, she could do so easily. But it is love and affection that predominate in the gentle barbs she throws their way. *"Putin's a zero, Zelenskiy's a hero"* indeed!

"I can't digest this war between Ukraine and Russia," writes Julia Gonchar in *A Sense of War,* a terse diary-like piece that slips into dramatic dialogues, memories, and dreams from time to time. She delivers a plethora of minute details — memories of mango and lavender tea that don't satisfy her as usual; the skulls of long-dead divers; fears of catching toxoplasmosis from cats; on to an actual, historical incident, the receipt of a text message from one of the writers represented in this collection: ". . . playwright Pasha Arie in our Theater of Playwrights group chat: russians (so written in the original — JFr) will attack Kyiv at 03, be at 02 at the shelter." Each of her observations is capable of painting larger, intricate pictures that may sound benign enough on the surface, but which, when taken together, become a tale of pain that is inextricably intertwined with sex, fear, and terror: "I push Seriozhka away, angry at him for touching my breasts, my genitals. I'm sick, I'm in pain, I want to scream. I know we may be apart for a long time. Happiness is stolen. [...] So war it is! Joy is stolen. It is my Devi Sorrow."

Pavel Arie, or Pavlo, as he calls himself, gives us the longest, most sustained narrative of all the texts. His *Diary of Survival of a Civilian Urbanite in Conditions of War* overlaps in form with many of them. Like Lagushonkova, he accompanies his text with photos. Like Astaseva, he specifically mentions the notion of a tale concocted in time of or in conditions of war. The diary form, with actual dates setting segments apart from one another, is used in at least half a dozen texts. Arie, like many, records the shock of those first hours of war.

But *Diary of Survival* stands apart for its reticence to be swept up in the twin madnesses of war and hatred. Not that they don't touch the author, they do. But Arie — whom we may equate with his narrator, for he assured me his text is factual — is skeptical of everything military, everything regimental, everything collective. He bristles against the limitations that his government and neighbors would force upon him, and he retreats farther and farther into his own personal world. He readily admits someone may not like what he says, but he stands firm. His purpose is to establish his own personal place in this mess that is war. He doesn't waste much time apologizing for that.

Planting an Apple Tree by Iryna Harets and *My Tara* by Liudmyla Tymoshenko both begin from afar before bringing narratives to the topic of war, the former being an almost bucolic tale of gardening, the latter – a meandering mix of history and memory.

The Tara of *My Tara* refers in name to the O'Hara family estate in *Gone with the Wind*, but in spirit to the home in which Tymoshenko's narrator grew up. The direct connection is made in the first paragraph where Tymoshenko's narrator recalls reading the story of Gerald O'Hara's funeral in Margaret Mitchell's novel (in Russian translation). Specifically memorable are Grandma's words as she tells Scarlett about "the sound of the end." These words will come back to give meaning to the narrator's own life experience, which is spread out over several decades in multiple countries. But from there, the story — which is more a biographical narrative than actual short story — moves on to tell the history of the narrator's life within range of potential nuclear war with a father who served in the Soviet Union's Strategic Rocket Forces, eating dumplings and cherries with her grandmother in Ukrainian summers, and retelling the tale of a grandfather whose extreme sexual arousal (and, perhaps, a bit too much moonshine) brought about the heart attack that killed him.

Tymoshenko quickly and abruptly pulls together the different lines of the family legends in the decidedly unsentimental final three paragraphs. The sound of Russian bombs ripping through the roof of her childhood home "was the sound of my Tara's windows being hammered shut with boards and plywood. It was the true sound of the end, for which I was not prepared."

Harets's *Planting an Apple Tree* also begins its journey from afar, but quickly orbits in close to the topic of war. The two topics — gardening and witnessing war — exist side-by-side uneasily in paragraphs that tend to butt up against one another more than flowing from one to the next. The jarring, nauseating, vile realities of war are entirely contrary to everything that goes into and comes out of nurturing a tree that will provide beauty and nutrition.

"Today, again, diarrhea and nausea," Harets writes. "I just went to vomit. But what about the apple trees? Aha, we must not let the roots dry out."

I held up the completion of this collection for several months, waiting for the final two texts to come in. One never did before the acting edition of this anthology went to press in early January 2023. Yevhen Markovskiy had been trapped in Kherson, a city that the Russians overran and seized in the first week of the war. The Russian-installed administration sought to make an example of the city, kidnapping and disappearing prominent professionals, intellectuals, and cultural figures even as the local population — at least early on — protested openly on the streets. Internet was frequently cut off, telephone lines worked sporadically, and life-sustaining supplies were scarce — in short, the city was thrust into a siege mode, Markovskiy along with it. He was in no position to write. As a precaution he removed himself from social media and erased all files in his telephone.

In the absence of anything from Markovskiy, we honored his position in the first iteration as one of the founding members of ToP with a dedicated page in place of the text he had planned to write. For the record, here is what we printed on page 245:

Yevhen Markovskiy had every intention of writing a short text for this anthology. He confirmed that in several notes over the course of four or five months. But I never received a text. Markovskiy was in the city of Kherson when it was overrun and occupied by the Russian army in March 2022. Despite the extreme danger, he remained there as the war dragged out to seven and then eight months. It was impossible for him to write under such circumstances. Then in early fall 2022, he removed himself entirely from social media, deleting everything he had written, including letters. This empty page stands as a sign that we are waiting for a text from Yevhen Markovskiy anytime he should choose to send one.

Wonderful news came in early February 2023 when fellow playwright Liudmyla Tymoshenko informed me that she was not only in touch with Yevhen, she had heard he had written a series of songs while holed up in Kherson. Sure enough, after a flurry of emails among Liudmyla, Nina, Yevhen and myself, a group of eight audio files showed up among my messages on Telegram. They were followed shortly by printed texts of the lyrics.

My first reaction to hearing the songs was ecstatic. They were brutally understated, hilariously deceptive, and incisively sharp observations of life lived in a city gripped by an enemy occupation. My second reaction was one of horror for, in a stroke of borderline deranged brilliance, Yevhen had recorded the songs as an exotic imitation of Tuvan throat singing. Moreover, these home recordings included the occasional background laughter of an attending female, as well as that of Yevhen when he was particularly amused by what he was doing. How would we make these aggressively muted, essentially tragic, yet always mirthful songs communicate on the page what they did so viscerally in the highly unorthodox recordings?

Once again, I turned to Liudmyla Tymoshenko. "Help!" I wrote. "I need explanations!" She began by offering her own astute commentary, although the turning point came when she sent Markovskiy's own detailed answers to my questions. I merely translated them and appended them to Markovskiy's lyrics as addenda. Voila! A fine ending to one of the most troubled and troubling aspects of compiling this anthology.

Maksym Kurochkin, like Markovskiy, was too fully engaged in war to write for the longest time. Kurochkin spent the first nine months of the war traveling among various hot spots as a member of Ukraine's volunteer territorial defense unit. For months he would write, "I am almost done!" or "I have just one page left!" or "I will send by this evening, or, at least, during the night!" As fate would have it, Maksym delivered his contribution precisely on the day in mid-November that Ukraine liberated the city of Kherson from the Russian occupation.

Kurochkin's *Three Attempts to Improve Daily Life*, like Oksana Grytsenko's *The Peed-upon Armored Personnel Carrier,* is essentially a finely honed short story.

At the same time it is, like so many other texts collected here, a personal and true confession. Its wistful humor and occasional lyrical moments are tinged with foreboding. Its deeply tragic aspects are understated and brief almost to the point of vanishing altogether. Its underlying currents of hope are colored with disillusionment. As hard as it is to believe under the circumstances, Kurochkin almost entirely erased the person who experienced these events, leaving behind only the laconic, crystal clear observations of a dry-eyed author bearing witness to truth.

LOOSE ENDS

Almost all of the texts contained herein were premiered in readings and staged readings as part of the greater Worldwide Ukrainian Play Readings project. As of this writing, 407 days into the war, we have organized 365 performances of 150 texts by 50 writers in 30 countries and 20 languages. I stress the fact that "we" have conducted this project, for it truly was a global effort, involving, primarily, William Wong and Amy Sze in Hong Kong; Elli Salo in Finland; Andreas Merz-Raykov and P.J. Escobio in Germany; Dominique Dolmieu and Ian Stephens in France; Ema Vyroubalova in Ireland; Raluca Radulescu in Romania; Romana Storkova-Maliti in Slovakia and the Czech Republic; Yevgenia Shermeneva in Latvia; Victor Marvin in Estonia; Bryan Brown, Neil McPherson, and Steve Hennessey in the United Kingdom; Alex Borovenskiy in Ukraine; Leslie Baker in Canada; and Robert Matney, Carey Perloff, Mark Seldis, Anya Zicer, Vladimir Rovinsky, Lisa Channer, Igor Golyak, Kate Bredeson, Amy Pinto, Rachel Vigour, Jenya Mironava, Sam Buggeln, Aoise Stratford, Charles Duncombe, Tim Habeger, and Philip Arnoult in the United States. And that is only a list of individuals who participated multiple times, sometimes in multiple countries.

Dominique Dolmieu introduced me to Nina Kamberos, founder of Laertes Press, the finest, most detailed, and sensitive publisher I have ever encountered. She became a true collaborating partner as we put this edition together. I am deeply indebted to the professional team of editors and proofreaders, Valerie Price and Margaretta Yarborough, who I am certain can find the tiniest of needles in the largest of haystacks. My hat is humbly off to them. Maxine Mills worked wonders with the graphic design, bringing some of these unorthodox texts to life on the page in ways I never imagined.

Translations for the Worldwide Ukrainian Play Readings were done by over 40 individuals. The vast majority of English-language translations were done by John Farndon of London, and by me, often with the aid of Natalia Bratus. Farndon, a well-known writer and translator, the author of over 1,000 books, translated two of the works in this collection (one with the aid of Evgenia Kovryga). I could not possibly have handled the workload of the worldwide project without John's enthusiasm and tireless work ethic, to say nothing of his talent. I am very happy to represent his work in this collection. I mentioned Natalia Bratus earlier in this introduction, and I would like to add that her stoic character, her readiness to work, and her attention to detail made every moment of work that we shared a real creative joy.

Throughout this anthology I referred to the 2020 decree issued by the Ukrainian government to standardize transliteration of Ukrainian into English (Transliteration). However, I did stray from it when common sense and/or accepted practice interfered. I allowed each writer to choose how their names would be spelled in English, regardless of "rules." Some are already known in the West under certain spellings, others use pseudonyms that require a loose approach, some didn't see themselves in the versions that the standardized table produced, others had quirky preferences that fell outside the mainstream (Natalia Vorozhbyt prefers to be identified via the diminutive Natalka). We discussed all the possibilities, and I deferred to each writer's wishes in all instances.

Some words and concepts that arise or recur throughout the texts require explanation.

• *Banderites* is the term used to describe Ukrainians who followed, or currently revere, the Ukrainian nationalist Stepan Bandera (1909–1959). He was a controversial figure, hailed as a hero by many in Ukraine, and labeled a terrorist by the Soviet state. He was executed extrajudicially in Germany, probably by poisoning, and his legacy is still used today in Russia as "proof" that Ukrainians are fascist nationalists at heart.

• *Ruscist, Ruscists,* or *Ruscism* are forms of a word that arose in connection with several wars involving Russia in recent decades — Chechnya in 1995, Georgia in 2008, and Ukraine beginning in 2014. As can be seen, or heard when pronouncing (rAshist), it is a combination of the words Russia or Russian, and fascist or fascism.

• The letter Z is occasionally used in unexpected ways for a specific reason. The Russians chose to use the letter as a symbol in many places, often on their tanks or personnel carriers, ostensibly to identify Ukrainian President Zelenskiy as their primary target. However, many around the world, and certainly in Ukraine, quickly pointed out that the symbol looked like half of a swastika. The irony of an army invading with the expressed purpose of defeating Nazis, while employing a Nazi-like symbol, was lost on few. Ukrainian writers picked up on that, giving us the rather satisfying derogatory combination of "PuZin" (Putin).

• As a pejorative reference to Russians, the term *Goat* or *Goats* has a long history in Ukraine. Some believe it was because of the long, pointy beards that Russians traditionally wore in the very old days, as opposed to the dashing mustaches that Ukrainians tended to sport. Also met are references to Russians as *Orcs*, and Russia as *Mordor*, both drawn from J. R. R. Tolkien's fantasy novels.

- *FSB/KGB* are terms referring to Russian agencies of state security. The FSB (Federal Bureau of Security) is contemporary Russia's successor to the better-known KGB (Committee for State Security).

- In the end I rejected a request from Maksym Kurochkin to write all words referring to Putin, Russia in any form (Russia, Mordor, etc.), and Russians in any form (Russians, Ruscists, Goats, Orcs, etc.) with lower-case letters. I felt the emotionally charged device drew too much attention from the substance of the texts, and, frankly, often made them look like they were filled with typos. I hope Maksym and the other writers will accept my apologies for making this decision. My purpose was solely to present their work in the strongest possible form.

At the end of March 2022, I spent an hour talking on Zoom with Natalia Korczakowska, a director who runs the Studio Teatrgaleria in Warsaw. She read several of the texts presented here and was impressed by the fact that all of them imply new ways of directorial interpretation. She saw in them nothing of the old-fashioned narrative drama that we are so accustomed to. In an email, she wrote that the texts "are realistic in a new way. They will inspire new theater forms of expression which we desperately need in our time of constant change." During our Zoom, she added, "They might lend themselves to street theater." Korczakowska said that not yet knowing that Anya Zicer would stage many of them outdoors in the woods in June 2022 at the JetLag Festival in upstate New York, or that in September 2022 Bogdan Saratean would place actors on residential streets of Sibiu, Romania, to surprise passersby with unexpected readings of texts about war, fear, anger, or that in early 2023 Rachel Vigour would take to the streets of Charlottesville, VA, to record selfie-videos of the texts in various local historical spots. Nor did Korczakowska yet know about the series of videos, often quite experimental, that were put together by various artists in numerous theaters in Germany from May to July, 2022. Although it had already been completed by the time we talked, she did not yet know the innovative short made by Myro Klochko and Anatolii Tatarenko of Andriy Bondarenko's *Peace and Tranquility* (not included in this collection, but available on YouTube). It would be a prize winner at the Kinosaray film festival in Kyiv in July.

Maksym Kurochkin hinted at the different nature, the newness, that these texts would possess when he refused to give me access to anything written before the war began. Obviously, he knew that texts written before the invasion might run the risk of responding inadequately to Ukraine's new circumstances. But Kurochkin had more than that in mind. He understood that the utterly extreme circumstances would require writers to seek out new ways through which to express their thoughts, observations, and emotions. That is what he meant when he wrote that he wanted to "retain control of the discourse." And he emphasized what he meant when he added, "That is important."

It is also important to remember that all of these texts were written by writers of a theater that, officially, does not even exist yet. That, however, does not indicate an absence of activity. As early as December 2021 there was a collaboration with the Münchner Kammerspiele, while after the beginning of the war numerous venues stepped in to offer support in the spring and summer of 2022. These included the Maxim Gorki Theatre in Berlin, the Royal Court Theatre in London, the Vienna Schauspielhaus in Austria, Teatr Dramatyczny in Warsaw, the film school in Łódź, the Polish Radio Theatre, and several other theaters in Poland and Germany. Still it was largely thanks to Maksym Kurochkin's insistence, and the generosity of Philip Arnoult's CITD and Noah

Birksted-Breen's Sputnik Theatre, that these writers came together to pool their talents and professional resources to begin writing a multitude of texts that would define the Theater of Playwrights before it even opened. The reading held on 24 June at the theater's future space in Kyiv was followed by a similar series of readings in early December 2022. These were continued steps in the building of the foundation of a theater that was still slowly coming into being. Kurochkin himself declared adamantly that these events did not constitute an official opening. That would happen, he stated, only after Ukraine had declared victory in the war with Russia.

And yet, the texts of this not-yet-existing theater have already struck a chord all over the world. Some have been read or presented 60 or 70 times. Audiences have attended readings in nine venues in France, 12 in Finland, 19 in Romania, 36 in England, 42 in Germany, and over 65 in the United States. This book is being published before the Theater of Playwrights has had a chance to open its doors officially.

What that implies is that this book is a sign of promise, of hope, of commitment, and even obligation. If anyone ever wants to know what Ukrainians were thinking, what they were experiencing, what fears and aspirations they harbored when Russia bizarrely chose to invade it in the late winter of 2022, this book holds answers. This book will do these 20 writers proud. When their people and their culture were under attack, when some dared claim they didn't even exist, they stood proud and laid down in their own words the parameters of a new Ukraine.

— John Freedman
Chania, Crete

April, 2023

Sources

Alessandro Achilli, "Four Decades of Modernist Revolution: Creating a New Subjectivity in Ukrainian Poetry, 1900–1940," Harvard Ukrainian Studies 38, No. 1–2 (2021): 111. *https://www.husj.harvard.edu/articles/four-decades-of-modernist-revolution.* Accessed c. 2022.

Uilleam Blacker, "What Ukrainian Literature Has Always Understood about Russia," *The Atlantic* (March 10, 2022). *https://www.theatlantic.com/books/archive/2022/03/ukrainian-books-resistance-russia-imperialism/626977/.* Accessed 14 November 2022.

Andrew Evans, "Who Really Owns Borscht?" BBC website (October 16, 2019). *https://www.bbc.com/travel/article/20191014-who-really-owns-borsch.* Accessed 14 November 2022.

Jason Farago, "Culture War, with Bombs and Missiles," *The New York Times* (July 18, 2022): A1. https://www.nytimes.com/2022/07/28/arts/design/ukraine-war-art-culture.html. Accessed 14 November 2022.

George G. Grabowicz, "Taras Shevchenko: The Making of the National Poet," *Revue des études slaves* LXXXV-3 (2014), 10 and 15. *https://journals.openedition.org/res/398?lang=en.* Accessed 14 November 2022.

Natalia Korczakowska, email of 26 March 2022.

Maksym Kurochkin (here and later), texts exchanged on Facebook Messenger, March to October 2022.

M.A. Meillet: *Anthologie de la littérature ukrainienne* (Paris: 1921). Available at: https://diasporiana.org.ua/wp-content/uploads/books/776/file.pdf. Accessed 14 March 2023.

Joe Mulhall, "'For now, music is a weapon': the Ukrainian musicians playing on as an act of resistance," *The Guardian* (8 March 2023): https://www.theguardian.com/music/2023/mar/08/for-now-music-is-a-weapon-the-ukrainian-musicians-playing-on-as-an-act-of-resistance. Accessed 11 March 2023.

Kelly Nestruck, "The Battle for Bulgakov's Nationality," *The Guardian* (11 December 2008): *https://www.theguardian.com/stage/theatreblog/2008/dec/11/mikhail-bulgakov-ukraine-russia.* Accessed 14 November 2022.

"On the Historical Unity of Russians and Ukrainians." Official Kremlin website, 12 July 2021. The official Kremlin translation into English is posted at https://en.wikisource.org/wiki/On_the_Historical_Unity_of_Russians_and_Ukrainians. Both sites accessed 14 November 2022.

Kvitka Perehinets, "Executed Renaissance: The Erasure of Ukrainian Cultural Heritage in the Times of the Soviet Union," *Retrospect Journal. https://retrospectjournal.com/2020/11/22/executed-renaissance-the-erasure-of-ukrainian-cultural-heritage-in-the-times-of-the-soviet-union/.* Accessed 14 November 2022.

Ged Quayle, Facebook post 31 July 2022: *https://www.facebook.com/photo/?fbid=10221026949567715&set=a.1124124707605.* Accessed 14 November 2022.

Transliteration table: *https://unstats.un.org/unsd/geoinfo/ungegn/docs/26th-gegn-docs/WP/WP21_Roma_system_Ukraine%20_engl._.pdf.*

A DICTIONARY OF EMOTIONS IN A TIME OF WAR
OLENA ASTASEVA

PART 1

Panic

I fly into my apartment and shout:

"Matvei! Quick, run to the store! We need to buy food!"

"Auntie, we have tons of food. I bought potatoes. There's more than enough for two days."

"Don't you get it?! It's war! What if the stores close for a week? Or a month?"

He can't imagine that. Nothing has ever happened in his 21 years that would have stopped him going to a store anytime he wanted to buy whatever he wanted.

Fear

They're bombing us. I hear the sound of shells outside the window. I google what to do.

"Hide in your apartment between two windowless walls. No doors, no windows."

I run around the apartment. I don't have any walls without windows or doors! Even the bathroom has a window. The corridor has three doors, and one of those has glass in it. What idiotic planning.

Maybe best to run to the basement? I go to Google again.

"Do not hide in basements under any circumstance if there is no water source, air conditioning, and a toilet."

We have none of that in our basement.

I lie down on the sofa. Nothing's going to help me anyway.

Hunger

You have to stand three hours in line to buy anything. But what do you buy?

Buy meat and freeze it? But if a shell strikes the electric grid, there will be no electricity and the meat will go bad.

Macaroni and grains? But what are you going to eat if they turn off the gas? You need something that doesn't have to be prepared. Cookies? They sold out long ago. There are none on store shelves. Dry out some bread maybe, but there's no bread either.

I look at the empty shelves in confusion. I've got to come home with something. Something we can eat sitting in a basement while bombs land on my apartment house.

Cleaning

I hate dust. I really should vacuum the place. But what if they bomb the apartment? Then why the wasted effort?

What if they evacuate us and we have to leave immediately? No point mopping the floors. Does one need to clean an apartment in a time of war? Does anyone know what the rules are on this?

Betrayal

I didn't understand immediately what was going on. Why were my cultured friends from Russia mumbling abstract phrases like *"I oppose war,"* instead of saying *"My government is committing a crime. It has been seized by evil forces. I am in despair and don't know what to do?"*

Just three people wrote that to me. That's probably quite a few, given that it seems every fourth inhabitant of Russia is not only not against the war with Ukraine, but even happy with it.

I always thought citizens of the Russian Federation were living people, but they turned out to be zombies.

What's most annoying is that my friends who quit communicating with Russians, and switched over to the Ukrainian language after 2014, turned out to be right. I wanted to be tolerant. I thought people were not to blame. It's all Putin. I didn't watch Russian TV. I didn't know what was happening there.

Exchanges with a Russian Girlfriend*

ANNA. How are you, Lena?

YELENA. Alive. The city is occupied. There's no way out.

ANNA. You asked me to write who among us Russians support you. I don't understand, how could anyone NOT support you?

YELENA. I do believe that not everyone in the Russian Federation is a zombie.

ANNA. I have a couple of friends in the Ukraine. Some have been very aggressive, some have quit writing altogether. My friend in Kiev saw a rocket out her window, and she unleashed an incredible tirade of aggressive accusations at me in a text as if I were personally to blame for that.

*Translator's note: I use Russian forms when the author engages Russians (Kiev, Kharkov), but I use Ukrainian forms when it's Ukrainians among themselves (Kyiv, Kharkiv). Note that Russian friend Anna uses the outdated form of "the Ukraine" — a form used in Soviet times when Ukraine was perceived as a "territory," or "district," not an independent place. This usage is now highly offensive to Ukrainians, but some Russians still cling to it.

YELENA. I understand her. When your home is being bombed, you feel hatred.

ANNA. I myself would like to understand.

YELENA. There are many dead and wounded. Kharkov is destroyed. Kiev is constantly being bombed. Many of my friends are refugees now.

ANNA. I couldn't have imagined anything like this happening in the 21st century.

YELENA. I'm afraid to go out of the house. Lines for bread are two hours long.

ANNA. The sanctions against our country are laughable. Half of Russia consists of backwater towns. Grannies in chicken coops, as I imagine it. So what's not working out there? Apple Pay? I'm going to go feed the chickens.

YELENA. It's like finding myself in a film about war. It's a nightmare. You go to bed, and you fear your home will be bombed that night. There's nowhere to buy food or medicine. And when you write about all this, your Russian friends answer that it's fake news. What do you think, how do I feel?

ANNA. The situation is complicated by the fact that I've had COVID for two weeks. I am constantly on different pills, wiped out entirely, and that makes it seem as though everything is a dream and I'll wake up any minute now. Such insane things can't possibly happen in dreams.

YELENA. I wish I could wake up, too.

ANNA. A blockade is coming upon us, too. It's informational for now, but an iron curtain is not far in the future. But I want to know the truth. I want to see it with open eyes, even if it frightens me. That's why I wrote you directly.

YELENA. Did you see the video of Kiev and Kharkov being bombed? That's all true — you need not doubt that.

ANNA. I'm afraid to watch Ukrainian channels. I can't stand so much pain and tears.

YELENA. Do you think we can stand it?

ANNA. My husband received an official call-up. He was very surprised. It said something like, "Just in case, you must be blah, blah, blah." He's like that. Okay, he's strange.

YELENA. Your friends and relatives will kill our people and vice versa. Then you'll start to feel hatred.

ANNA. Don't worry, my husband couldn't kill a cockroach.

YELENA. If Putin orders him to, he will.

Hatred

When you hear the sound of a shell flying at your house, at first you feel fear, then hatred. Hatred for whoever did it. For all of Russia, for all its inhabitants without exception.

When there is silence outside the window, your brain kicks in, and only then can you rationally think about things.

Until you hear the sound of a shell outside your window, you will not understand what hatred is.

Love

I have a friend. Well, not so much a friend. The relationship is complicated. He lives near Kyiv. I live in Kherson. We rarely see each other.

He used to text me every morning:

"How you doing, babe? As fucking awesome as ever?"

Now I write him every morning:

"How are you there today? Any shooting? Are you still alive?"

We had decided that each of us was on our own. No obligations, an open relationship. Now we discuss how we will live together when the war is over.

"You will work, and I will stay home and cook," he jokes.

"The hell!" I say. *"I'll lie on the couch and read all day. And every evening I'll retell the stories of books to you."*

He wanted to come to Kherson on Women's Day, March 8. But the war began February 24, and now I have no idea whether we'll get together or not.

I'm afraid one day he won't pick up the phone. The place where he is now is under heavy fire.

Exchanges with a Ukrainian Girlfriend

MARYNA. A woman was killed in the next house. I have no windows anymore. We're escaping now.

OLENA. Maybe someone will help us get out, too. But where?

MARYNA. I had no plans to leave until an hour ago. Now everything has changed. I took almost nothing. The cat is howling. Lena, pack your suitcase. Don't repeat my mistakes.

OLENA. What city are you in now?

MARYNA. Rubezhne. Fifteen kilometers from Sievierdonetsk. Sievierdonetsk is being shelled heavily. My job is gone. Shells keep hitting our neighborhood. I've already written off our apartment building. How are you doing?

OLENA. We're under occupation. No food or medicine have arrived in the city since the war began. We're threatened with starvation if this continues. For now we're finishing up what we bought before the war. The city authority has not changed yet. The Ukrainian flag is still flying. But the mayor was ordered to forbid the residents to do several things — drive a car, go out after 8 p.m., leave the city.

MARYNA. They have begun killing the leaders of the territorial defense here. I have no job anymore. Shells keep hitting my block. I already said goodbye to our building. I want to leave. I don't know what to do with the cat. Basically, I'm totally confused. And it's not so easy to leave because of the shelling. But I'm scared as fuck. I am still shaking after a shell fell 20 meters from my house.

OLENA. An entire family here was shot up in their car on their way out of the city.

MARYNA. I want to escape, but my brain is overloaded... Home, mom, the cat. To say nothing about the fact my boyfriend will be mobilized — that's obvious. He will stay here. He plans to join the territorial defense. Unfortunately, we aren't married. We put it off all summer. First we remodeled our apartment, then we traveled, then we were swamped with work. I didn't really want to get married officially. I thought, who needs it? But now... How will I look for him later if I am not his wife? I only hope he survives. And what's the point of me staying here if all the men are being conscripted? Our apartment is unlikely to survive.

But what about our cat... Lena, I can't just leave him on the street...

Irritation

I read the posts of those who managed to escape. They're in Europe now, safe, and I am very happy for them. I follow their stories: some in Poland, some in Moldova, and some in Sweden. I understand it's difficult for them abroad. But it irritates me for some reason. It's the desperation of being trapped.

Guilt

I feel guilty when I read about Kharkiv and Mariupol. Because these cities are being bombed heavily. Our Kherson didn't suffer much: a shopping center, two apartment buildings, a few schools. We're kind of outside of things because everyone else is fighting while we are under occupation. This is the guilt of the soldier who has been taken prisoner.

Messages from Friends

1

I've had no contact with Mother since the morning of March 2. She is in Mariupol. All communications are cut. It's war. All I could find out as of today: no one has had gas, electricity, or communications and food for a long time. Her apartment house was bombed. People cook porridge on a bonfire in the courtyard. I hope she is alive. I believe she is fine. I'm waiting. Waiting is very hard. I'm powerless, but I believe.

2

Today I stumbled home from the hunt with three loaves of bread and two packages of oatmeal. My sister, dad, and aunt conducted a special operation on apples and brought home a pack. There is no fruit. And I need vitamins. I stood in line as explosions went off around us. Fuck it. A kilometer from my house they're digging some kind of ditch. At the airport four kilometers away, we hear explosions at night. I spend all day on the Internet, probably like everyone else. I'll give birth soon. The main thing is to have access to the maternity ward and medicines. People write every day from different cities and countries — come here. Oho! More noble madmen . . . We are under occupation — where am I going to go? I keep kicking myself for not leaving. Not for my sake, but for my future baby. I'm very pessimistic about the end of all this shit. That's life. One day at a time.

3

Day Twelve of the war — how are you doing? Everything is fine here — planes flying over, explosions, my legs are killing me from standing in lines for food and animal feed. We have enough to eat for another five days, then for a couple more days we will eat pickled cucumbers and drink fruit compote.

I'm exhausted. I try to read, but I really can't, especially when explosions keep distracting me from my book. I am counting on the army — I donated all my spare cash to them in order to hasten our victory.

Choices

What you can die of during a war:

If a shell hits you, it rips you to pieces.

If a shell hits your apartment building, you can be crushed under the rubble.

When a shell hits, a building might catch fire. You might burn up or die of asphyxiation.

You might be shot in your car as you try to leave town.

You might die of hunger sitting in a shelter because you can't go out for provisions.

You might die of hunger because there's a blockade and no food is delivered to your town.

You might die of thirst if your water system is damaged and there is no water.

You might die of illness because medicines are not being delivered to your city.

Time

As soon as war began we said:

"It will last a few days and then it will be over."

Then:

"It will all be finished in three to four days."

Then:

"We'll know what to expect in two weeks."

Two weeks passed, and now I hear:

"This war was planned to last a month."

For some reason I have bad premonitions.

Weather

As I woke up this morning I heard thunder in my sleep. I thought, "It's going to rain."

Then I came to fully and realized — those were shells exploding.

Kherson
12 March 2022

Commissioned by a grant from Philip Arnoult's Center
for International Theatre Development

PART 2 EVACUATION

Sensation of Loss

"Auntie, why are you saying goodbye to me forever like that? We'll see each other in a month! The Ukrainian Armed Forces will free us soon. Are you crying?"

"Matthew, come with me!"

"I'm not leaving Ukraine for anyplace. I am on my own land here. You go, you'll be safe there."

Where am I going? Why? Does anyone care about me there? I pack my things as if I were hypnotized. What should I take?

"Don't take clothes. They'll give you clothes here," my sister writes to me from Europe. "Take your favorite things — it helps."

I want to take my favorite pillow, but it won't fit in my backpack.

News from Friends

1

Kherson is no longer our city, the one we lived in. The atmosphere is that of a prison cell. I plan to leave.

Today I packed into a single sack everything I had acquired for an entire life.

I know I will be lost wherever I may go, and I will be super unhappy there. I am still connected to my past life here, but there I will have to come to grips with everything that is happening and discover inside me the strength to live on. I am terribly afraid of this, and so I keep putting off my departure.

2

Russian soldiers at checkpoints search phones, bags, and your car. Smashed cars lie on roadsides, there are minefields all around. They made me take off my clothes so they could see if I had any nationalistic tattoos. Boy, do I look like a Nazi (not).

The half of the village by the road is brutally battered. There are no phone poles. Wires lie across the road. They pinched my telephone power bank from me . . . I say they pinched it. In fact, a drunken soldier with a machine gun asked me for it, and somehow I didn't have the courage to refuse him. Sorry.

We pass a checkpoint. The Russians ask us where we're going.

"To Mykolaiv."

"Don't go there. We're going to wipe it off the face of the earth in two days," one of the Orcs at the checkpoint advises us, as if offering friendly advice.

Anger, impotence, a forced thank you for worrying about us and pedal to the metal as we zigzag through a minefield they planted for us.

3

I was in depression, it took a week or more afterwards for me to come to my senses and return to a normal life. But even now I can't call this normal life. I'm constantly on the phone, or scrolling through the news, or waiting for some call from occupied territories.

I fear for my relatives. I'm afraid this will last until the new year, and that the Russians will plunder our house in Kherson. They visited our parents in the center, and they were at our house, too. But that's probably the least of my worries.

In fact, my whole life was stolen from me. This understanding comes to you when you try to make yourself at home in a new place. Our old cat won't even go outside. Everything is unfamiliar to her here. She no longer wants a new life . . .

4

My daughter asks me:

"Mom, why can't I go to my own school? Live in my own home? Go to my art school? Play with my girlfriends? Sleep in my own bed? Why did they take all that away from us? Why won't grandma come visit us?"

What can I say?

"Be thankful you were not killed on the way, that our car was not strafed, that neither your leg nor your arm was ripped off, that you were not trapped under rubble, that your family is alive, and that we are safe . . ."

"Rejoice, sweetheart!"

And now she is crying.

Bitterness

I go into a gas station cafe. I want to grab a cup of tea for the road. To leave Kherson I had to go through hostile Russian territory. This is the first stop.

I see content, cheerful people. These are Russians. They don't have the letter Z branded on their foreheads. They have no horns nor hooves. They sit at tables, drinking and laughing. Chocolates, buns, and cakes are all around them on shelves. Everything looks beautiful, and it's inexpensive.

In my city right now storefronts are bashed in, shop doors are boarded up. Right now people stand in lines for bread in my city. Tanks and armored personnel carriers drive through our deserted streets. Sounds of gunshots and explosions are heard.

I want to yell at these people. After all, it is THEIR country that is at war, it is their FAULT. I feel tears well up in my eyes. I leave the cafe without drinking my tea.

De-realization

In Europe, everything has a doll-like sensation. As though I have found my way into a fake world filled with toys. The streets, paved with stones, are too clean. The houses are too small, and too beautiful.

I stare at these sweet little houses with their panoramic windows. I imagine bombs falling on them, their glass shattering.

In Europe, everyone is too relaxed, too carefree.

I somehow want to shake them up, make them understand . . . That we Ukrainians are not just some special people you can bomb. This might happen to you, too, one day.

"Rockets fell in Kyiv again today," I say.

"Are there still women and children in Kyiv? I thought there were only soldiers there. I don't watch the news anymore. It's too hard."

Tears

I almost never cried before the war. I didn't cry over books or sentimental films. There was no reason in my life to cry.

"You are the happiest person I know," my friend Sasha told me.

I cried for the first time when I saw a burnt-out shopping mall in my city. It was hit by a rocket. Firefighters wanted to put it out, but their truck was shot at.

I have had many reasons to cry since then. I cry when I read the news.

I cry when I hear the song "The fact of the matter is I have no home." I cry angrily when I see contented, well-fed Russians, while their country destroys mine.

I cry when I see women in beautiful dresses. All of my dresses were left in Kherson. I know this is a very silly reason to cry.

My friend Sasha, he's a music lover. He collects records.

"I heard music for the first time since the end of February, and I sobbed as I sat next to the player, listening right to the end of the track. It didn't feel any better," he writes.

War is when even men cry. They can do that now.

PTSD

I leap up in the middle of the night from the sounds of explosions, and rush to the window. Did war really start here too?

Have the Russians come here too? But no, it's just fireworks. For someone it's a holiday.

I flinch when a plane flies overhead. I interpret the loud rumble of a motorcycle as the rumble of a projectile.

When I enter an unfamiliar house, I automatically look for blank walls with no windows or doors. Or, at least, does this house have a basement?

Does your house have walls with no doors or windows? Check it out. Where will you hide when bombs start falling on you?

From Correspondence with a Russian Friend

ANASTASIA. In fact, I am quite ready to believe that "not everything is so clear," that you really do have Nazi battalions somewhere, and that there is convincing evidence that the people of Donbas have suffered from this for eight years.

ELENA. We don't have any Nazi battalions! And the people of Donbas have suffered for eight years from a war that was unleashed by YOUR country! And this is all QUITE CLEAR!!!

ANASTASIA. You know, I don't understand politics much. I lack the erudition to engage in arguments. You believe your TV, we believe ours. My husband says we'll figure it all out when it's over. But, naturally, he and I oppose the war.

ELENA. If you oppose it, why do you do nothing to stop it?!

ANASTASIA. What can we do? This regime is designed in such a way that no one is able to oppose the tsar. Thousands of people attended rallies in the first days of the war. Many of them are still in prison. Long terms have been imposed for "spreading fake news."

Yes, we are all to blame for the fact that we only voiced our opposition in our kitchens. But we have lived our lives, and we wanted to live them. Only heroes are capable of laying down their lives in the battle for justice. I'm not a hero.

ELENA. But we must stop this somehow!

ANASTASIA. I really want this to end as soon as possible, too. But Russia is full of bastards who are ready to kill everyone for 200 thousand rubles a month. I don't know when they will be no more. In any case, it is obvious to me that only darkness awaits us.

ELENA. It seems to me the only thing a normal person can do in this situation is leave. Everyone who remains in Russia will have the blood of Ukrainians on them. Leave!

ANASTASIA. Personally, I'm not planning to go anywhere. My husband has a job, a good position, and it's stable here. Anywhere else we would have to start all over. No one cares about us anywhere. I understand people who leave because they cannot remain in a country that . . . on the other hand, I don't understand why I should have to completely rebuild my life because of the political leadership's stupidity. Presidents come and go. (I mean, they do go sometime, don't they?) But my country, my family remain.

Disillusionment

Many say now that they have become disillusioned with humanity.

I became disillusioned with humanity a long time ago — when I first read about the concentration camps and the Gulag. It was then that I realized: If it happened once, it can happen again.

I often hear the question: *"How can this happen in the 21st century?!"* The century isn't the point. People are not getting any better.

Scientific fact: People's brains have not grown over time, but shrunk. We are dumber than cavemen.

People are stupid, naked monkeys. With nuclear weapons.

Anger

I didn't know I had so much anger in me.

I am angry:

- at Russians, because they turned out to have rotten souls.
- at the Ukrainian government, which allowed this war to happen.
- at the Europeans, who could stop it, but are too cowardly.
- I am angry at Macron, at Scholz, at Zelenskiy, and the Lord God. At those who switched over to speaking Ukrainian, and at those who did not. At those who left the country, and at those who stayed behind. At those who continue to have faith, and at those who have already given in to despair.
- I am angry even at myself, although I don't know what for.
- I give in to anger so it won't hurt so much.

Arithmetic

Twenty-two thousand civilians were killed in Mariupol. I am now hiding from the war in the Irish town of Wexford. The population of Wexford is 22,000 people.

Imagine for a second that your entire city is dead. Imagine that everyone you know has died. Imagine that all the houses in your city have been destroyed.

By the way, how many people live in your city?

Three hundred thousand people lived in my hometown of Kherson. One hundred and fifty thousand of them left because of the war. They all live in different places now, scattered everywhere. They have nowhere to go back to, because Kherson is occupied.

Imagine that you left, and you have no place to go back to.

Forty-four million people live in Ukraine. Six million left the country. The rest live in a state of war.

By the way, where will you escape to when war comes to you? I hope you have a reliable plan.

From Correspondence with a Ukrainian Friend

In my picture of the world, Ukraine balances on a line of separation between good and evil. Europe and America are in no hurry to supply weapons so as not to anger the schizophrenic Putin. Otherwise, in a fit, he might destroy all of humanity in an atomic conflagration. Of course, they won't let him seize Ukraine, but they don't want to deliver him a crushing defeat either. Along the way, they stall as they wait for sanctions to devour the Russian economy, so that Russia itself will abandon this unprofitable crazy fraud of a war. Then Ukraine will remain intact, and the Russians will be sated. For all this we pay with our lives every day.

Emptiness

One day I started scrolling through the news about shelling and deaths. One day I chose not to look at photos of destroyed houses.

One day I saw a photo of a dead child and I didn't cry. One day I didn't read the news, turning on music instead. One day I wanted to watch my favorite TV series again.

One day I wanted to forget about the war forever. One day it seemed to me that I would never feel anything anymore.

Despair

People here ask me all the time:

"How are you?"

And I answer:

"I'm fine, I'm good."

I know this is accepted here, and that you should smile.

But I'm not fine, and I'm not good at all.

Every morning I learn about new deaths and destroyed homes. Every time I feel like a piece of me is breaking off, too.

Expectations

I no longer expect to hear the news that the war has ended, as I expected to for the first month. All the same, I'm expecting that, in another month or so, it all will end. It's impossible for this horror to last long. But the impossible lasts and lasts and lasts . . .

Faith

We now have the Ukrainian Armed Forces in place of God. I believe in the Ukrainian Armed Forces. I believe that good will be victorious. I believe in our victory. I believe that Moscow will be destroyed, and that the bunker dwarf will disappear. I believe that all Russians will see the light and repent. I believe that Russia will disappear from the face of the earth.

I believe that Kherson will be liberated, and that all my friends will return. That one day everything will be as it was before. That we will gather again at my friend Sasha's to play board games. We will drink tea and listen to music, everything will be as usual.

Sasha will say:

"You will win. I believe in you. You are tenacious."

"It's just that I don't like to die," I will answer him as always.

The last time we played board games was during the occupation. Sasha is still there in my city that has been desecrated by the Russians. There are no jobs, no money, no medicine, communication lines do not work. People there are still waiting for the return of the Ukrainian Armed Forces.

Sasha last wrote to me:

"I know you'll be fine there. You're tenacious."

I believe we will see each other again one day. You can go crazy if you don't believe.

Wexford, Ireland
16 June 2022

JFr

CALL THINGS BY THEIR NAMES
TETIANA KYTSENKO

A war-ning.

When I was a teenager, my family lived in the small town of Zhdanivka in the Donetsk region. The city of Zhdaniv was 200 kilometers away, on the shores of the Sea of Azov. Confused tourists heading for Zhdaniv regularly arrived at our bus station in Zhdanivka. In 1989, Zhdaniv was renamed Mariupol, and we seriously discussed whether we might change the name of "Zhdanivka" to "Mariupolivka." That never happened. But in 2017, Marshal Zhukov Street, where I lived in Kyiv, was renamed Kuban of Ukraine. Around this same time, the street named for the January Uprising of 1918 was renamed in honor of Ivan Mazepa, while Moscow Prospect was renamed after Stepan Bandera. In those years, there were still many renamings going on within the framework of decommunization — villages, streets, metro stations — and at first it was confusing and annoying. But the new names took root: because they are OURS.

Honestly, I would rename many other things: "Soviet champagne"; "Zhiguli" Russian beer; "Russian" cheese. Being a rational person, I would advise these manufacturers to change their names urgently: otherwise their products will just spoil in warehouses because those names will get stuck in everyone's throat. (As I have been writing this text, "Russian" cheese was renamed "anti-Russian.")

Then there are a number of cases where renaming is a debatable issue. For example, Putin for Hitler. After a detailed study of the issue, I don't believe they should be equated.

The Nazi leader was incompetent, but an artist; he at least had some traces of taste. Before plunging his people into an abyss, Herr Adolf managed to paint a convincing picture of the future. Finally, in defeat, he had the courage to lay hands on himself. True, only after the fall of Berlin, but still, that wasn't bad.

As a zealous officer of the FSB, Putin possesses not a single hint of creativity. He never speaks a word of the future — only about the Great Past, and not even of the Soviet period, but of days when toilets were a hole in the ground. You find yourself listening to the demented delusion of this old man — and you realize: the hell he will lay hands on himself. No, he'll throw nuclear bombs at the entire world. Wouldn't you say that Putin is worse than Hitler?

The immutable Russian president is a monkey playing with a nuclear button while sitting on a gas tap. For the safety of everyone, this three-pronged entity must be disassembled forever.

To be honest, I didn't believe until the last moment that PuZin's Russia would attack Ukraine. But when my husband and I leapt up at 5 a.m. on February 24 from the sound of exploding cruise missiles, we knew what was going on even without news reports. Was this a "Special Operation," a "conflict," or a "crisis?" No, not one of these words came to mind. And if such "diplomatic definitions" are rinsed of their hypocrisy, you'll have the old standard: "war."

War is when you're going west through Hostomel and a downed helicopter catches fire right above your head, and you rejoice because it belongs to the enemy. It is when you sleep in the bathtub at night, wake up from the bombs, and feel the walls vibrating. It is when you live in the subway for four weeks, know how to distinguish "Grad" rockets from bombing strikes, but don't know if your house survived. Also, when your relatives from Russia say it's all fake.

How did it happen that calling things by their proper names became a civic feat in Russia, Belarus, and a few countries in the West? Why is the truth so overvalued? It seems so obvious to declare war a war, criminals – criminals, and heroes – heroes. It is important to name the number of dead, captured, and even those Russian soldiers who refuse to return to Russia. After we try them for the crimes they committed, let them rebuild what they destroyed – then, maybe, they can remain with permanent residence status. If they're willing to learn Ukrainian.

Of course, everyone in Ukraine will understand Russian. But will a Russian understand anything here? I remember in 2007 a journalist from St. Petersburg, Sasha, came to work in Kyiv for a Russian-language publication. For a couple of weeks, he complained how difficult it was for him. The last straw was when Sasha went to do an interview and spent an hour looking for Red Banner, or Krasnoznamennaya, Street, not even guessing that he was walking on it. After all, the street signs bore a radically different name, Chervonopraporna, that is, Red Banner Street in Ukrainian. (Incidentally, it is now called Pirohovsky Lane.)

Russian soldiers thought if they got into trouble, they would be able to blend with the crowd in any Ukrainian city. But we all remember how the locals, seeing a man with a shaved head and wearing someone else's clothes, shouted at him: *"Hey, say 'palianytsia!'"* that is, "breadloaf" in Ukrainian. But a Russian simply can't say this, because Ukrainian requires different adjustments of the oral apparatus. Language has become a password, an identifier, our Identification Friend or Foe system.

But here's what I think: Even if a Russian understands the language, will they really understand Ukrainians? It's not even a matter of the meaning of the words, but what stands behind them. Take, for example, our leading national virtue — "sincerity." It's not just a matter of being "frank." It is an odd fusion of cordiality and breadth of soul mixed with frank honesty — the ability to call things by their proper names. I would require exams to prove people know such things.

By the way, about names: I've noticed one interesting nuance. It's not so recognizable in everyday life, because I speak both Ukrainian and Russian. But when corresponding in English, I have noticed feeling irritation when foreign colleagues address me not as Tetiana, but rather by using the Russian version. My dear friends, Tatiana is something else entirely. The difference of one letter is enough to embrace an entire worldview.

JFr & NB

Commissioned by a grant from Philip Arnoult's Center for International Theatre Development

THE PEED-UPON ARMORED PERSONNEL CARRIER
OKSANA GRYTSENKO

It was around 5 a.m. that war broke out in a village at a crossroads where nothing ever happens. At first the dogs barked, then explosions were heard. They were firing somewhere from the direction of the headlands. Villagers ran from their houses, scratched their heads, and asked where they could find a bomb shelter. Someone said there was one at the school, but no one knew who had the keys to it. So everyone went back to their houses and decided to just sit on their butts.

A few hours later, a column of Russian tanks roared down the main street which was once named for Lenin. Naturally, there were heavy trucks, armored personnel carriers, oil tankers, and other such crap. The column ripped up the town's asphalt roads well into the evening. And over the next days too. Some villagers jumped in their cars and headed north. They left no trace, while those who remained in the village (that is, almost everyone) decided to just sit on their butts, and not stick their heads out. Especially since checkpoints had already been set up. The village was surrounded and occupied.

Fighting broke out around midnight, but the villagers just huddled around their houses. Because who would know where to run, and, here, there were neighbors all around. It's more fun in crowds. Then everybody broke up, and in the morning they went to work. Those who had work, anyway. Russian flags were already flying in the town center, the mayor was missing, and half the shops were closed. The villagers rushed to stock up on bread and flour, and hid their expensive cars in gardens and barns just in case. Meanwhile, that night, two brave souls pulled down a Russian flag.

The first thing to disappear in the village was bread, followed by medicines in pharmacies, and then Ukrainian national television. After that, the Russians (in this village they were always informally called Goats or Butchers) stripped the mobile communication wires off the TV tower and planted landmines around it. The villagers felt as though they were stranded on an island, cut off from the world. They walked around their village with their mobile phones, turning them here and there, looking for those cherished lines of communication. The dashes did not appear on their screens. The mayor never showed up.

There was milk, however, which farmers began distributing for free. Because there was no way to leave the village to sell it, the cows were still producing milk, and you can't just throw milk away. Then the Armenians began baking bread, the Turks brought in vegetables, and other farmers brought in meat. The shops were completely empty, but the villagers always knew where to get what. As such, despite all the predictions, no humanitarian crisis had yet occurred.

Next the townspeople buried Ukrainian soldiers. Three were found on the edge of the headlands, and several more in a molten tank, where only bones were left, so no one ever found out how many died there. For the longest time the Goats from Muscovy would not allow burials, but finally the priests from the Moscow Patriarchate persuaded them to allow one. It was the only one to take place in the village.

People carried coffins and flags down the main street, the one that used to be named after Lenin, the one along which the Russian Goats had entered the village. They buried the bodies nearby. The armored soldiers were dumped in a common grave marked by a sign, "Unknown Defenders of Ukraine." The Goats watched all this from their vehicles, moving slowly through the countryside. They did not walk on foot; they tried not to let the villagers see them.

Meanwhile, Wi-Fi, then mobile communications unexpectedly returned in the village. Russian channels ran on TV, but the villagers had long been using satellite dishes, so they watched whatever they wanted. Naturally, they got their news itself from the Internet. And on the Internet people were writing that Ukrainian flags were flying in the surrounding towns and villages, that people were capturing Goats in the bushes, were stealing their armored personnel carriers, and refusing to eat their humanitarian aid. The villagers scratched their heads and fell into thought.

The next day, they took flags and placards and went looking for Goats, shouting *"Glory to Ukraine!"* Damn, everybody all around here is giving us the eye, the villagers thought. What the hell are the Goats doing here, anyway? It will be harvest season soon. This is Ukraine, after all. And there never was any love lost for the Goats here.

At first the villagers approached city hall and knocked, but the occupiers were not there. Only the poor mayor appeared, stiff with fear, and he disappeared again. So the villagers headed for that same old former Lenin Street to look for Goats. They found their tents and armored personnel carriers in the bushes on the village outskirts.

There were several hundred villagers and about a dozen Goats. Both sides were a little scared. But the villagers took the upper hand with their daring, their shouts, and their numbers. They shouted *"Putin's a Zero! Zelenskiy's our Hero!"* and demanded that the Goats leave. The villagers were not sure the Goats understood, so sometimes they translated *"Dodómu"* – "Go home!" in Ukrainian – into *"Domói"* – "Go home!" in the language of the Goats. The Goats refused to come out of the bushes. So the activists climbed up on an armored personnel carrier. They jumped on it, shouted, and waved a flag, trying to break it. But nothing would break. Eventually, two brave souls solemnly peed all over it.

The Goats would not move and the villagers all went home. Because it was already evening and they had to feed their chickens and ducks, to say nothing of having to think about what to do next. Because this was already the tenth day of the occupation, and not a single person in the village was sure that they would live to see morning.

JFr & NB

Commissioned by a grant from Philip Arnoult's Center for International Theatre Development

HOW TO TALK TO THE DEAD
ANASTASIIA KOSODII

Yesterday I saw four photos of Ukrainians who were killed by Russians.

The first was a gray-haired man who was being lifted on a board from a mass grave. His pants were down to his calves. His chest was swollen.
The second was a woman with long dark hair and a red jacket. Her arms were crossed on her chest. Lilies of the Valley rose up to the right of the woman. To the left was earth plowed by explosions.
The third was a black body bag, not fully closed. You could see a man's head with an open eye, his gaze frozen.
The fourth — this girl was alive. But she had no left cheek and part of her jaw was missing. Everything was red.

At night I lie down and recall doing an interview near Kyiv with an artist who is now exhuming bodies. *"At night,"* he said, *"I sometimes hear sounds. I don't fear them. They are our dead. Let them come. They died so badly. I, at least, will talk to them."*

How to Talk to the Dead

How do you talk to your dead
I think you know
no special workshops are required
we determine our dead as a fact of life not of death,
tragic as it may be, we tell stories about them,
we at least try to imagine them, an apartment in a new
building in the suburbs of Kyiv surrounded by parks and
pine forests
minibuses from the Arsenal Metro Station
The Sea of Azov alongside the silhouette of a
metallurgical plant
vacations to salt mines to breathe and restore your lungs
local champagne that is impossible to drink
the communist Artiom who came down
off his pedestal on Central Square
visits to the hairdresser for hair care procedures
an ice palace for sports, performances, and competitions

school number one, school number two, school number three
ammonia-free long-lasting cream coloring
3-1 dark brown hair color
oat milk for conditioning.

tasks for the future
invent stories
so that your dead will speak through them
about the life that has taken place and has yet to be
outstanding
eccentric
unforgettable
ordinary people
the way they wanted to be
I think, how long might it take
to begin

no one promises

you will do everything right

don't waste your time searching for

the form

for words or speech, and

suddenly

there will be such words as have never been

it's never been this bad

history wrote itself justly

enemies gave rise to sunflowers

your people

were alive

as they

wished to be.

JFr & NB

SURVIVOR'S SYNDROME
ANDRIY BONDARENKO

THE END

Every one of us was killed
already that morning.
We are no longer
what we were then.
We died.
On February 24
of the year 2022
a neighboring country killed
us all.
The old world went up in
flames and smoke, splintered
and disintegrated.
Hundreds, thousands,
millions of our worlds
disappeared, destroyed
forever, irreversibly.
That week I had decided to
go on a date. Winter was
coming to an end, but it was
still gray and cold. I wanted
finally to change something.
We made a date for the day
after tomorrow, February 24,
the year of 2022. We were to

meet in the center of town, sit at a cafe, walk the streets. That day, the day after tomorrow, never came. Something else entirely came about and ruined that day. You think you want to go for a walk?! There was no city in which to meet and have a coffee. There were no more streets. Something else entirely happened. Other lives of other people now. We'll have to become acquainted again, set a new date, meet at another time. Everything will have to be reassembled, piece by piece. And the pieces themselves will be completely new. But when will that be?
Who will I be?
Who will we be? Where will we be? What will our purpose be?
The Apocalypse has come. Everything that was
is no longer.
What remained were vestiges, shadows.
We used to watch TV series,

drink beer and cognac. We stayed out late at coffee houses, visited friends, bought paperback books, hugged, talked about art, played cards, laughed, danced to music on our phones. We went to the movies, drinking beer and eating nuts.

This all disappeared one gray cold morning, swept into the dark abyss by the sound of an air raid siren. This is how worlds disappear. Like a day that ended and never came again. Like a flower that clamped its petals shut under a gust of wind and never opened again. Like a laptop suddenly disconnected from an outlet. Like a sun that set in the west but never rose again in the east. Like a man stabbed in the heart from behind. This is how worlds disappear — like a light bulb going out, like water draining from a bath, like eyes being shut on a dead man's corpse. Our world was no better than

a light bulb. Just as fragile and finite. That's how it turned out. Our world was imperfect. It was alive.
It was killed.
The Apocalypse now has come.
There is no fear.
That which we feared is now long gone.
Traces, remnants, shadows — we have retreated to another side, an Atlantis beneath the surface of the sea. We still see it, but the image grows weaker.
Our life now is a graveyard of all the plans, desires, and aspirations that we had before February 24, in the year of 2022.
We now live in a world in which our world no longer exists. How can that be? It just is. That happens too.
Forests through which we used to wander are mined, and devastated by tanks. Bridges we used to take to visit relatives are destroyed. Our relatives are dead or

gone crazy. Friends are held captive in captured cities, or have left for where they never had any intention of going. Theaters are bombed to dust. Theater actors guard checkpoints with machine guns in hand.
What kind of world is this? This is a world of war. And what is war?
It is something that cannot be. Ever. But it is. How can that be? It cannot be. We live in a world that cannot be. What could not happen has happened. The unspeakable has happened, the unreal has happened.

Are we alive at all,
we who survived?

Who am I now?
How did I survive those first days? I remember little. Those days are already buried under some big, impenetrable pillow. All we did was wave our arms as if they were wings, so as not to

fall into the abyss that our lives had become.
It turned out we had wings — those of us whom we now have become.

I still don't understand — where are we? We are in different places at the same time, like ghosts. Like foggy clouds, we fly wherever our thoughts lead us — to where our friends, family, and loved ones now sit in basements, shuddering from rocket attacks, or just frozen in fear for someone's life.
We now hover over all of Ukraine like ghosts. Our bodies obediently remain where we left them. We are only half of our bodies, or a third. We are carried here and there by the invisible winds of war.

Our bodies are like children. We command them to be polite and obey their elders. Sit still, hold this backpack with documents, carry us onward, until our thoughts and souls carry us to those who are dying beneath the bombs.

Where are we? Our places and spaces have been replaced, spread out, confused. Train stations function, but they are no longer train stations. Cafes function, but they're not cafes. People sit and drink, but that is no longer drinking. A drunken friend called me recently. He was sitting with another friend. His friend had a bottle. They both got drunk. My friend got very drunk, sat there drunk and happy, listening to music on his phone, remembering funny stories, and then he went home and suddenly woke up. He remembered everything. Dark, empty streets surrounded him on all sides, and his windows were taped shut.
A territorial defense patrol stood under the bridge. My

friend called me. *"What should I do*, he asked, *I was drunk, I had fun, and suddenly I woke up. There's a war going on. It's very scary. There is a patrol under the bridge. Why did I get drunk? What's so fun about getting together with music and funny stories if there's a war going on?"* "Don't worry about it," I said. "Just hang up and go home quick. Curfew starts in five minutes. You'll be stopped by a patrol.
And you're drunk." "Damn," he said. "Curfew! And I was so happy half an hour ago when I was drunk!" "Go home quick," I said. "And don't drink anymore." "I won't, I won't, fuck, I won't," he said and hung up.

Those who have no tomorrow should not drink vodka. It's pointless. After all, your hangover will come today. It won't be postponed 'til morning. We have no tomorrow. There is only one big, swollen today. Heavy,

gray, swollen clouds spread
over the entire horizon, in all
directions, filling all the
cracks.
No matter how much you
drink, you'll still come back to
this today. Nothing lies
behind the gray clouds. The
road to the future is gone. It must
be found again, just as
we look for... What? For nothing.
Finding your future is finding your
future, nothing
more.
Who knows how to look for
it? We must learn this from
zero, from scratch, from the
emptiness of the day's
eternal gloom.
Just as we learned to fly over
the abyss by the power of
wings we previously did not
have.
Hanging over the abyss
bifurcates or even trifurcates
you.
I went for a walk. It was
around mid-March, a bright
high, dazzling blue sky, the
warmth of the sun falling on
shrunken faces, caressing

them like a mother's hand. A light breeze blows, children's laughter wafts in from somewhere. And your body responds, it responds to this spring around you. Your gait relaxes, a faint smile appears on your lips. But it's just your body — you yourself don't respond. A smile on one side of your mouth, sadness on the other. Like an ancient mask.

On the one hand, you absorb spring, but on the other, it is not spring — it is a battlefield, a fiery death. Combatants with machine guns now run beneath the big, blue, dazzling sky, the warm sun illuminating an enemy tank hiding near a ruined cottage. A car with refugees is shot up beneath this sun. People buried under concrete walls are dying in the shadow of this sun. Tanks, helicopters, cars, people, the earth are all burning beneath this sun with a transparent fire.

As such, you see around you two suns, two skies, two springs. You are here and there all at the same time, you are bifurcated, trifurcated, for some part of you is neither here nor there, but hangs at this moment over the dark abyss, the abyss of the Apocalypse. You now have three heads, for you must watch two suns and one abyss at the same time.
But you have just two hands. And they must carry you like wings.
Your world is destroyed, you are dead, you are flying somewhere, a stranger in every world on which the sun now shines.
You still breathe, but you know not what that means. I breathe — so what?
Am I still breathing? Am I breathing for now? Am I breathing already? Did I inhale? Did I exhale? Is this a pause, or is it the end, or the beginning? Who can say?

At this very moment the Ukrainian mathematician Konstantin Olmezov sits in a Russian prison.
He specializes in additive combinatorics, a field of mathematics that studies finite sets and their relationships.
When, on February 24 in the year 2022, one finite set in which he was currently located attacked the other finite set to which he belonged, Konstantin Olmezov could not believe in such a new relationship between these two sets, nor could he accept it as a fact of mathematics, or as a fact of life, and just two days later he both believed and wished to escape the finite set in which he was located at the time, but it was too late, and on his way in the bus he was arrested because he was recognized. Some element of his present finite set handed him over to the police, and the police arrested him for

the simple reason that he wished to escape from the finite set in which he was located, although that was no crime, and yet, they still imprisoned him, because he had said out loud that one finite set was wrong to attack another finite set.

Now Olmezov sits in a prison cell, hanging over the dark abyss. He sits and sits and sits. He sits some more, then sits more still, sitting, sitting, sitting, sitting, sitting, sitting, and sitting . . . But stop! No more! No more sitting.

His hands could bear it no more.

Konstantin Olmezov, a Ukrainian mathematician, detained and imprisoned in Moscow for trying to go home, committed suicide while in a prison cell.

At least that's what the news said.

His wings could not bear the weight. More precisely, they were clipped.

Thousands are falling into the abyss at the moment that I write these words. Why do I write about the mathematician Konstantin Olmezov?
Probably because he had been there, in someone else's finite set. It is much more frightening than here. Although I don't know that. It's scary everywhere. At the precise moment that I write these words, people in Mariupol are praying not to die deaths as horrible as their neighbors have already died. They want to die instantly. They have no doubts that they will all fall into the black dark pit to which they currently cling. Their spring right now consists of nights spent living underground, without heat, without food, without water. Their spring consists of days of death under bombs, days of burying corpses beneath the entry to a high-rise building.
The Apocalypse continues.

The Apocalypse is constant.
Apocalypse now. Today.
Already.
There is no tomorrow.
My world is gone. I have no
sense of life. I am carried
away by an invisible wind. My
body is as obedient as that of
a child sitting in a safe space
in a basement, or between
two load-bearing walls,
carrying a backpack with
documents and money. With
obedience and fear my body
waits for me to return from
the fiery spaces of spring,
where people are dying,
people dear to me, though I
don't know them all, people
who no longer have the
strength to fly above the
black abyss, whose limbs
have been cut off, who
fluttered like wings to the
bitter end in the emptiness of the
Apocalypse.

But arms and hands
are not wings.

Why do I go back, why do I still see the sky and spring, why do I hear the air raid alarm and go outside to buy bread, cabbage, and tomato paste, why does the sun still caress me like my mother's warm hand on my face, why does the right corner of my mouth rise in a strange half-smile? I have no idea. This is a strange thing, one of those that is already happening in the Apocalypse.

For example, no longer are there kilometers between Lviv and Mariupol, 1250 kilometers. There are corpses. The distance between Lviv and Mariupol is 1250 corpses of civilians and that is only according to official statistics today, which always underestimate everything, so as not to taunt the Apocalypse, so as not to look it in the eye.

In fact, there are many more corpses. We understand that perfectly well, but I do not tell that to my body, which

obediently sits where I tell it to sit. The body does not need to know everything. Let it think it is alive. But I know a terrible secret — we are not alive, we are flying over an abyss, for our world was killed and we are carried here and there by invisible winds blowing between life and death.
I can move my body where distances are still counted in kilometers, where it is still spring and not a fiery battlefield.
But the hot winds will reach me there too. I shall see the dark abyss every time I close my eyes, even if I just blink for a moment.
My world is gone.
Sleep, body, sleep. It's not easy for you either. You truly suspect something. After all, you smile with just one corner of your mouth, you wake up every day at dawn because you hear the ghostly sound of a siren, you do not taste food,

you fear blinking so as not to see the darkness I do not tell you about, dear body, so that you won't forget that you must breathe. For I have forgotten about that for a very long time. Because on February 24, of the year 2022, I found myself in a place where there is no air, where there is no atmosphere — it all had disappeared as if it had never existed, the sky went black as an abyss, even in daytime, let alone evening and night.

The first and last panic attack in my life came when, on the fourth day of the war, I returned home in the evening and looked up at the dark sky — and did not see a sky there. At all. How could a sky be there? Were there a sky there, Russian bombs and missiles could not fly through it. It would hold them back. But they do fly there, so there must be no sky. It is gone. No world — no sky. What could it cling to? There are no iron pillars, no green forests, no cherry orchards. I stopped, puzzled, my breathing stopped, I was bent low like grass, only my legs moved on and in that way I did not fall, but rolled on. When I rolled up to the wall of my house, my body began to breathe again. But I do not.

This combination, "is not," holds a certain magic for me, I repeated it over and over so that at least something will be. If you repeat "is not" a thousand times, it is as if there is something there, at least some crumb of dust that you can hold onto.

I love street sparrows and even pigeons. I feel solidarity with them. If they live, so can I. If the sun shines for them, then maybe it does for me? Maybe I'll catch their sun if I don't have my own. Maybe their sky will cover me a little, at least a little?

Sparrow sky! Cover me and all those I love. Think about and remember all who fly with me into the black abyss. We are like those sparrows — we fly, although we do not know how. We are like those sparrows — we die by the thousands, in the dust and ashes, homeless, restless.
Sparrow sky! Chirp-chirp-chirp!

Memories of those who were and died still swirl about me like dust. But there are fewer and fewer of them. I don't remember living the first three days of the war. An impenetrable pillow. That is, I know how — I sat in front of a laptop screen, unable to break away from the news. I posted hysterical appeals on Facebook, I called people, I questioned and passed on important information, forced myself to fall asleep, listened to the siren at dawn, started to read and immediately threw the book away,

experienced despair and love. I know it all – but I do not remember it.
What about who I was before the war? I know him – but I don't remember him. All I know is that it was someone else. He went to the bathroom differently, lived in my house differently, spoke differently, looked out the window differently.
He was and he disappeared. God be with him. I haven't time for him now.

Mariupol.
Bucha.
Hostomel.
Irpen.
Vasilkiv.
Sumy.
Okhtyrka.
Chernihiv.
Izium.
Popasna.
Volnovakha.
Kharkiv.
Kherson.
Mykolaiv.

Bashtanka.
Voznesensk.
Makariv.
Chernobyl.
Energodar.
Donetsk.
Luhansk.
Crimea.
Bakhchysarai.
Dzhankoi.
Simferopol.
Sevastopol.
Melitopol.
Berdiansk.
Kramatorsk.
Slaviansk.

These are the words I remember now. Which I will not forget.
I will not forget anything or anyone. Nothing and no one. Nothing that happened in the dark and in the fire. This is my sole bridge across the abyss now, and absent me already.

Therefore, yes. I whisper these words before bed.

Mariupol.
Bucha.
Hostomel.
Irpen.
Vasilkiv.
Sumy.
Okhtyrka.
Chernihiv.
Izium.
Popasna.
Volnovakha.
Kharkiv.
Kherson.
Mykolaiv.

...

These are word-cities. In them live all the people who have died, who disappeared, who were left homeless. This is my geography now. I do not know what will happen next. I know nothing, as my friends the street-sparrows know nothing. But I am sure of one thing — we will forget nothing. Nothing that happened. Ever. We shall remember to the depths of our bones and blood. Until we're calloused and full of holes. To the sparrow sky. As those remember who have nothing but this to remember. From whom everything else was taken away.

Thus shall we traipse through the Apocalypse now.

This is not a memory of us who came before, of those who lived, died, and perished with the old world. God be with them.
It is a memory of wings, love, fearlessness, and burning pain.
It is the memory of what happened when there was nothing left.
When we were ghosts.
When the dead were alive and the living were dead.

This memory is what we are now.

To hold it, we must build a new world.

And we will build it.
And there will be a new sky
over it.

We shall remember everyone
killed, every house
destroyed, every street
destroyed, every motionless
face.
We shall watch TV series,
drink beer and cognac, sit
late into the night at coffee
houses. We shall visit friends, buy
paperback books, hug
each other, talk about art,
play cards, laugh, dance to
music on our phones. Go to
the movies and drink beer
with nuts.

But before that I'll go on a
date.

...

And it will not be me.
Not the one who survives.

It will be the one who will be.

Who will live.

Who will remember.

Who will love.

Who, ultimately, will despair.

THE BEGINNING

JFr & NB

A TOPOL-M ROCKET FIRED AT A CAT NAMED BROOCH

LENA LAGUSHONKOVA

In the basement, my husband shows me a photo of a Topol-M rocket marked with the letter Z, and says it is coming at us.

Topol-M —
The Topol RT-2PM is a strategic complex with a solid propellant, three-stage ballistic missile.
Charge power — 0.55 megatons

Then he fell asleep.

The basement hears the howls of:
1. three cats
2. two dogs
3. four children

The rats here don't howl — they're local.

Mom does not shout. She is nervous. She wants to go up to the apartment to put the soup in the refrigerator.

A rocket lands in the neighboring yard. It did not land there on purpose — it was shot down.

But it's unpleasant all the same.

I fall asleep on the ground, but I wake up at five, because I can physically feel that a Topol-M is aimed directly at me.

I eat earth.

It's disgusting. But it makes me feel better.

To distract myself, I browse my Facebook feed.

It's still targeting me with anti-cellulite cream.

How many calories are there on Earth?

From the page of Aliona, a volunteer at a zoo:

A POST

ALIONA. I understand, but not really. Whatever. Is there anyone left in Hostomel?

A cat has been locked in without food and water since February 24. Its owner left for just a day but could not return. Address in personal info.

> Write to the Hostomel groups for volunteers. You can open the apartment.
>
> What about looters? That's against the law. Martial law.
>
> Horrors. There is a church in Hostomel.
>
> Whoever goes in, the cat will be frightened and hide.

ALIONA. I don't think she'll hide — it's been a week without food.

It's worse without water.

She knew all this. Why is she posting it only now???

> Do a search. Organize it yourself!
>
> Hostomel is a dangerous zone now. You might risk your life for the sake of a cat, but the locals aren't coming out of their basements to risk being shot.
>
> When they evacuated, people crawled on their bellies, shooting going on around them.

ALIONA. You think I don't know? I would still take the chance. I'm writing to those around me. Why do you write these things? To make me stop asking for help for this unfortunate kitty?

> I'm from Hostomel. Four volunteers carrying food were shot dead there yesterday.

ALIONA. I'd prefer you cuss me out with obscenities.

> I didn't mean to offend you. There are Russians. Kadyrov cadets from Chechnya. They go into houses.
>
> There are people in the basements!

ALIONA. I'm looking for PEOPLE!

Aliona, don't be angry. It's hell there. Shooting, explosions. There is no food, no water, no light. Freezing temperatures.

ALIONA. I understand. But there must be someone nearby! Just open the door! You can't pass by silently!

What about the shelter in Borodianka?

There are battles going on there.

Yes, it's impossible to move there! Kadyrov's Chechen cadets are flattening everything that moves!

Hello! I heard what the mayor said about the beginning of the evacuation of Irpen. My cat's there. Brooch. I am alone in Poland. Please take my cat — I can't!

So, you left your cat to die, but expect people to stick out their necks, right?

You piece of shit.

You should have taken it with you.

You don't know what to do about animals, but you go begging yourself.

They take them all in. Even the Russian ones.

Bitches. For every Russian one taken in, a Ukrainian is rejected.

But the mayor said — you can all get out! This is the last trip out!

> **ALIONA.** I blocked a guy from Poland.
>
> She's dead.
>
> **ALIONA.** Who?
>
> Your cat.
>
> **ALIONA.** I don't understand. Is this new information?
>
> My mother in Bucha is dead. Why should your cat be alive?
>
> Girls, friends! Everyone's nerves are frayed! Let's be kinder to each other — there's a war on. We have to find a good solution! Glory to Ukraine!

And they did find a solution. They knocked a hole in the wall, gave the cat food and water. An old, half-blind woman now takes care of it. She refuses to leave town because she just planted seedlings.

I fall asleep again.

My husband wakes me up. He says the Topol-M is fake news. Because why write a Z on it if equipment like that is available only in Russia?

You can go up to the apartment and go to the toilet.

Then come back down to the basement again.

A month ago, I signed a petition to condemn two people who terrorized a cat named Kuzia to spite their mother. They punched its ears with a stapler, and wouldn't let it eat.

That was in Omsk.

Omsk is Russia.

I do not want Russian cats to suffer.

That's the limit of my sympathy.

When I go to the toilet, I take off all my pants in turn — I wear several in case there's an explosion and I have to run for it. On the news I saw that an animal shelter is on fire in Markiv.

Video: Something burning is running.

Those are cats and dogs.

Battles rage in Markiv.

Rescuers will not approach them.

I have been safe for a few days. I only have two pairs of pants on, and I can take them off.

I find I have cellulite.

The TV is advertising pet food.

I don't understand everything — it's not my native language.

But the context is that everyone is happy.

https://youtube/uPi6Lh6wpkA

I don't know if I agree with what Adorno said about poetry,* but something must be done about the advertisements for animal food.

9 March 2022

JFr & NB

* "To write poetry after Auschwitz is barbaric." Theodor Adorno, 1903-1969.

Commissioned by a grant from Philip Arnoult's Center
for International Theatre Development

A SENSE OF WAR
JULIA GONCHAR

Before the war, we were in Egypt, in Sinai in Dahab. That's when I started writing these texts.

21 February 2022

I don't have cancer. I don't have HIV. But I'm constantly frail, with alternating phases of good health. Yes, I know I shouldn't write like this. I don't even have to say "no," because the brain doesn't perceive, doesn't perceive, doesn't perceive "no." Can't sleep, can't sleep, can't sleep! I dream in the morning of a host in a suit on the TV. I can't fix my attention. I fall into mindless wandering around shops. I persuade my friend to buy an expensive Adidas sweatshirt for 2,000 grivens.

In real life, it's the 21st — February 21, 2022. And I'm finally writing these rotten lines, getting down in words these weak intimations of despair. My stomach aches, gnawing away softly. On what? I can't digest this war between Ukraine and Russia. The 150,000-strong army at the border doesn't drop nicely into my stomach along with pieces of delicious shawarma or ripe mango, sweet and juicy.

I can eat nothing but plain rice, a plate of rice, nice rice. I'm just catching up on the news. I'm missing in action again. The rice drags out the slag and the water from me. And although the water is wide, the whole Red Sea, it is drowning me with waves of waterless anxiety. Why red? Filled with blood? Like menstruation? Three days later, and Putin has not attacked. A gray-haired general out with his troops says to the camera, *"We're stuck here in the cold. We're hungry on plain rice. We don't care about Ukraine's war on the Orcs: 'Why does Ukraine matter?' I'd be better off on a stingy liquid on the mattress with my Anastasia. I'd be better off eating shawarma and swimming in the Red Sea. I'm sick of this shit."*

I program, program my brain into that layer of reality where everything is fine, where the host on TV wakes me up. Putin is on TV. A speech. *"Give me a vesper martini! No need for vodka. No need for a sea of blood! Get away from me!"* "Leave, leave" as we sang in the anthem for our old Russian-speaking gymnasium so that we raised Pushkin's name in our hands to new existential heights. Our janitor-neighbor from the ground floor used to call it *gamn*asium — from *"gamno,"* shit. My mom and dad were always making fun of her. They used to warn me that I'd also end up a janitor if I was too lazy to study properly. It turned out that their family added a king-size balcony and sold the apartment for the office.

Russian aggression: My family is broken. In fact, no one is left alive but my aunt in Moscow, and she has cancer. I miss the dog Athena the most. A bull terrier, the best creature in the world. She's afraid of cats, because she was once beaten up by a mother cat — a fearsome sight, rearing up on its hind legs, swinging its claws, screaming, and inflicting such injuries that now Athena is afraid even of kittens. Athena also has cancer. Now Putin recognizes Luhansk and Donetsk as independent republics. Putin is moving his troops into their territory. And all the time I eat shawarma, absolutely filling my stomach, smothering the weakness. And all this is happening while I am eating . . . Everything will be fine.

25 February 2022

My boyfriend is talking to his father on the phone. His father is lying in Kyiv on the couch on one side of a high-rise building and refuses to go to the bomb shelter.
S's father. Your family is growing. You will have children. Your fiancée will soon be your wife.
Seriozha. I'm not interested in all this. I told you what I would do.
Seriozha's sister. Maybe you'd better stay in Poland? Or at least in Lviv?
Seriozha. Why are you still bullshitting with me?

Two weeks before the war...
I had a dream that a Russian or Belarusian soldier at a demo snatched a weapon and started firing at the crowd, I was just a hundred meters away. I thought: I have to lie low. Lying there, two women came. At 00:20, they went down to the subway. I didn't want to see the corpses. But I looked and there was already a boot shop, fake Doc Martens for 100 grivens, different as stockings for advertising boots. I thought: Well you need cool models for a beautiful shot. And I forgot about the war.

I remembered that I dreamed of my reflection. I did not like myself. I was different, fatter. The pain gets better then worse in my lower back. I can bend, then I feel pain again. I think it's psychosomatic and I need to meditate and dream. I dream that a woman gave birth to a watermelon pumpkin after holding it close to her belly.

A few days before Seriozhka's departure...
Me. And then you'll come back and we'll have a baby.
S. Aha.
Me. We just have to get married first because I won't do it otherwise. Then we'll have a baby.
S. Aha. Yes, Yulechka.

One and a half weeks before the war...
After coffee, I had a fucking dream. I fell asleep at about 5 and before that I was mesmerized by my heart beating like an express train and feeling on the verge of a panic attack. After a break, I drank coffee again. It had a bad effect on me. Yes, I became more talkative, but it made me feel like a hunted gazelle... I meditated quite ok, but then I listened to myself and only heard the thumping of my buffalo muscle heart. Soothing lavender tea did not help. Today was a strange day — in the morning I dreamed of bath-like coffins in which bearded men were laying along with some young girls, their daughters. *"If he married me, I would give our father tsar an heir — handsome, brave, beyond compare."* I thought about this phrase, which was taught at school on an empty stomach.

Seriozhka did not like it when I bought a pair of "unnecessary" glasses: some with heart-shaped red lenses, others with clouds and teardrops. Today Seriozhka threw cats over the fence, Lepeshka stole the cake again, and in the restaurant nearby there is an Arab man looking very much like that weird, bearded man from the theater festival in the village of Podvirne near Khmelnytskiy. The one who guzzled vodka, smoked cigars, then tried to clamber on the balance board showing us half his hairy ass.

I dreamed of the pine needles scent, Pepsi-Cola, Marlboro red. Serve more ammunition, the skulls of the divers who are already dead.

I have the best hairstyle now — long enough to feel the hair and short enough not to worry about styling. Although I never cared about it except in my school years.
S. Biden says Putin has already made a decision. There are already some explosions in Luhansk.
Me. And which country can you live in without a visa?
S. None.
Me. Well, maybe we can be sheltered somewhere.

Militants of the People's Republic of Luhansk (LNR) fabricated videos showing that the civilian population should be evacuated, published two days ago. Neighbors from London are celebrating a birthday and Kurt Cobain is playing very loudly. People in Luhansk are blowing up gas stations to accuse Ukraine. Bazhenchyk (S) is nervous. So am I.

Don't show me the way up to heaven; I don't need it. Yet. My relatives are already there. My aunt with cancer lives in Moscow and I can't jump there.

Today on the 19th we went to the Blue Hole. I'm on a tricycle, S on a normal bike. The scariest thing is that he . . . I'm afraid to even think, I'll persuade him to run away! Yesterday there was an outbreak of anger at S in bed, I beat him and I was so pleased to slap him with a toy owl — probably because of the fruit (strawberries and fezalis) in my bloated stomach.

The storm came that night. There was anger at Putin. Ben Marcus calls the most dramatic stories *"stun guns."* He says they hold you *"paralyzed on the outside but very nearly spasming within."* This is my stomach.

Today, February 21, 2022, I fed the goats with grapes and mango leftovers. I really liked it. At night, S told me a dream that he did not want to tell: I saw the child and thought, I will do one like this for Julia, I will fuck her without a condom. But during the day he changed his mind, and I had fears about toxoplasmosis from so many cats.

Today I finally wrote half a page. I liked it, and then we went to eat shawarma obsessively and compulsively. My stomach stopped hurting when we ate Syrian shawarma (everything was boiled and grilled, tomatoes and onions), and drank yogurt, and read tweets about what Putin said in his speech accusing Ukraine. Then we watched the Japanese film *A Man without a Map.* There were some very funny moments, namely the framing idea — unusual, mirrored, with constant daydreaming cutaways — something strangely like Fassbinder (the illusion and the main character). After the shawarma, we sat, and I cried.

S. Oh fuck — two Turkish private planes are taking off. People are running away.

We sit together and watch the movement of planes, a "military operation" is announced, a denazification. I'm going to take a shower.
S. Maybe he will attack only these areas?
I come out of the shower naked and warm.
S. He is bombing Kyiv.
I'm crying hysterically. I fall on the bed. He tries to comfort me. I see moisture in his eyes, for the first time. I'm glad he finally cried. At what price! I'm still sitting with

him, watching the news in his Telegram group, crypto wolves. Tired, I go to bed with earplugs. I can't sleep.
S. I'm going to join the territorial defense.
I'm in despair.
Me. And me?
S. And you come with me.
Me. No. I don't want to. I'm not going. I am a coward, a miserable pussy.
Video call with Sveta in the morning. Sveta with a cigarette in her Kyiv apartment, holding her chihuahua Maniasha under the armpit. Sveta is sitting behind the sofa, fenced off from the windows. One can hear the bombs.
According to the secret information shared by the playwright Pasha Arie in our Theater of Playwrights group chat, russians will attack Kyiv at 03, be at 02 at the shelter.
S. Valhalla! I want to be a warrior. A Viking.
I'm super scared to be alone.
Night from 27 to 28 February 2022: We fly to Germany from Sharm el-Sheikh. At the airport in Egypt, only one man is in a mask. A dude with a fag in his teeth at the check-in desk. The place is filled with cigarette smoke. There is no smoking room, so everyone smokes everywhere. I want to smoke. Camel yellow or Marlboro red? Nothing better than a Camel. I remember the taste of cigarettes. So disgusting and so pleasant and familiar, emanating in my '90s childhood from kiosks and the markets where my parents sold jeans. I got angry many times today. At the airport, I was mad at the dudes who selectively check bags. It bothered me. Germans were not checked, just us! One policewoman in a hijab sang to distract herself from the pleasant procedure of touching my tits searching for something. Now the dude has turned on music on his smartphone, and everyone is listening. He stands next to me, hugging his jacket. This Arab man can cry. Seriozha sits alone, constantly reading the news on Twitter and Telegram, glad that I moved away. We ate the most expensive panini — 150 Egyptian pounds for one, 10 bucks. The flight was diverted. To Germany, Cologne. I haven't been there yet. This is a surprise: we had intended to look at the Sphinx, but in the end, we are going to look at the Cologne Cathedral. There are many Ukrainians, and I greet them with *Slava Ukraini!* Glory to Ukraine! then check, listening to their pronunciation. I was angry with the taxi driver

that Seriozha had agreed to pay 50 pounds. The taxi driver was saying: *"It's for one!"* So persistent. Bazhenchyk spoke, argued, and I shouted, I shouted!

Me. Yes, we have a war on, and you greedy Egyptians just demand money!! He fell back. Like the one who wanted to check the suitcases, fell back when I shouted. I text with Bazhenchyk's mother and tell her that I want children. She says we are also very much looking forward to grandchildren.

We slept the first night in Cologne — vegetarian diet, we were well fed by Mario and Karin — muesli, then pasta with mushrooms, peas, and asparagus.

I dreamed that I'm stuck with a bad guy who hurts me.

Me. Why do I need you?

Bad Guy. I'm your stimulus!

I remembered this word very well. For the second time I dreamed that my friends were going to celebrate my birthday. I run away from everyone, go down the stairs, with Bazhenchyk behind me. I want to go out because I feel very tired. I see people carrying gifts.

God, how good it is when there is no war!

Wine. But I'm so tired I don't want to celebrate. I want to go home!

Today we are in the great cathedral of Kölner Dom. Last night, we slept in the second-floor bedroom. Karine is engaged in cognitive-behavioral therapy. Mario is a media artist.

S. Where is your paper bin? I don't need these contracts anymore.

Mario. Are you sure? I can save them for you.

S. It has to be signed by the producer, but it will take some time.

Fatigue is felt in the head like a helmet, a Kevlar helmet. Suddenly the heart beats, or somewhere below, at the level of the genitals, the center of pleasure.

It is gone for now. In the morning I push Seriozhka away, angry at him for touching my breasts, my genitals. I'm sick, I'm in pain, I want to scream. I know we may be apart for a long time. Happiness is stolen. We eat cheese with truffles. Mario and Karina have Irish cookies with milk from cows grazing on grass. We try to joke. We go for a walk in the park and S runs towards a hanging rope. I say to myself that if he manages to pass — the war will end. But he does not pass; he jumps on. So war it is! Joy is stolen. It is my Devi Sorrow. In Mario and Karina's flat, there's a poster on the wall with the inscription "Don't fall in love with your suffering!"

In the cathedral Seriozha takes photos of everything, and I sit on a bench and meditate, watching the thoughts in my head. I rest my feet on a stool, very comfortable. Around the scenes of Christ's suffering, his wounds healed, displayed to the audience. I was rather more impressed by the pixelated stained-glass window of 2007 and the planet Saturn in bright orange. I meditated and thought.

Me. I'm comfortable now, and I don't have to stand as in Christian Orthodox churches.

I remember the warmth of my fur coat, which can transform itself into a midnight blue leather coat. I can feel its downy softness on my skin. I am ashamed that instead of praying for peace, I am thinking of my fur coat, now hanging in the wardrobe in my apartment in Kyiv — if the house hasn't been blown up by Russian peacekeepers yet.

S. Take your feet off the stool — they are for praying on your knees. That's how they do it.

He quickly knelt, then stood up. I slowly pulled myself up on a wooden rail and became firm. Suffering. We are flying to Poland.

S confused the time and instead of 23:50 we are departing at 21:50.

I'm finishing yoga. My friend Andre dropped by with his girlfriend, also Ukrainian. We eat curry fast.

Me. I'm sorry, I had to finish yoga. I have to keep the rituals. It matters to me.

I'm shaking at the table. I tremble and talk a lot. Karin gives me 150 euros. I say this is a very awkward situation. I take it.

2 March 2022: A volunteer in Poland is looking for ammunition and a bulletproof vest for Seriozhka.

Me. [*Cries*] I can't let you go.

S. Why do I need that armor?

Me. It will keep me calmer.

S. Well, if I have a bulletproof vest, I'll enroll in the shock troops — otherwise I'll be sitting at the rear.

5 March 2022

Before he left we had sex without a condom for the first time.

JFa & EK

Commissioned by a grant from Philip Arnoult's Center
for International Theatre Development

ROBINSON
VITALIY CHENSKIY

01.

Robinson. A few days ago I finally decided to stay in Kyiv. At the time that I write this text, Russian troops have advanced in the southeast, set up a stronghold in the Borodianka area, and are gradually encircling the capital from the west and south. After the news of the utter destruction of Kharkiv and Mariupol, this is, shall we say, rather worrying. On the other hand, no matter what Ukrainian city you go to, Russian troops may come there too. Then again, you have to go somewhere. Maybe even abroad, someday. My ex-girlfriend has lived in the Netherlands for ten years now.

Ex-Girlfriend. Over this time I have acquired a firm opinion about emigration.

Robinson. And what is your opinion?

Ex-Girlfriend. Well, that it's very hard to do anything. People really don't consider you human. You are isolated as you move forward. No one wants to be your friend.

Robinson. I see.

Ex-Girlfriend. You don't cry about it. You pull yourself together, and do what needs to be done.

Robinson. What?

Ex-Girlfriend. That's a kind of slogan in emigration. You don't cry, you pull yourself together, and do what needs to be done. Although you want to cry.

Robinson. I see. I'm staying. Basically, one's chances of remaining alive aren't that small. I sealed up the windows and stocked up on water. I can sleep in the corridor.

02.

Chris. So, my mother calls and wakes me up and shouts into the phone: *"It's war, it's war! Let's go buy groceries. You don't have a fucking thing!"* I get the kids up immediately: *"It's war, it's war!"* The children howl with laughter. We go, and find lines a kilometer long. I try to get into the cheap supermarket — like, I have kids, and all. But they don't let me in. They do let us into the Megamarket. They say: *"Come on in, Mom."* We triumphantly grab a bite to eat at the cafeteria. I guzzle down some beer. I grab a whole basket of groceries, but I have no cash, can you imagine that?! And the ATM isn't working! I'm stuck in this Megamarket now. I don't know what to do. The girls and I agree to . . . In short, I'll tell you when I see you . . .

Robinson. I think that's the last thing she said to me as a normal person. After just a few hours of war, Chris turned into a wheezing, croaking loudspeaker, spitting out: *"Bitches! Fuck! Putinist rats! You won't succeed! Choke and die!"* and things like that. It is said a man always is uncomfortable alongside a crying woman. I would say it is harder to be around a woman burning with hatred for her enemies. If she does pay you any attention at some point, she'll have a question for you: *"Why are you still here and not on the front lines?"* Well . . . I can't offer Chris an answer to that. That's why I don't call her anymore.

03.

Robinson. I've been living alone for two weeks now. Most of my time is occupied reading news on the Internet. However, I had to think about what I'd do when the electricity goes down and the Internet disappears. Sitting in the dark doing nothing will drive you crazy. So I came up with the idea of reading books by candlelight. I already bought a box of Polish candles at the market and found my beloved Dostoevsky in my bag. So I will light the candles, sit on the bed in the corridor, and open up *The Village of Stepanchikovo and Its Inhabitants*.

Dostoevsky. They planned to start a family game of whist; but these games usually ended with the General suffering such seizures that the General's wife and her retinue lit candles in horror, offered up fervent prayers, told fortunes using beans and cards, went to hand out bread buns in the prisons, and anxiously waited for the afternoon hour, when, once again, they would organize a game of whist, for which they suffered screams, squeals, curses and even almost beatings for every mistake that was made. The General, when he didn't like something, was never shy before anyone: He squealed like a woman, cursed like a coachman, and sometimes, ripping and scattering cards on the floor while driving his partners away, he even wept with annoyance and anger...

Robinson. At that very moment, a Russian rocket flew in my apartment window... Not the most subtle plot twist, of course. Rather mediocre dramaturgy. But, in general, there will be nothing better in the coming years.

04.

Dana. Don't panic. Keep calm, everything's all right.

Boria. How long will we be there?!

Dana. We'll wait a little then come back. We'll take a watch...

Boria. But we just got back from the shelter!

Dana. No, Boria. That was this morning.

Boria. And we were there all day yesterday!

Dana. It wasn't all day. We arrived at night. Because it was dangerous.

Boria. It wasn't just at night! We were there all evening too!

Dana. I know you're upset, Boria sweetheart, but that's how things are now.

Boria. How are they?! Why! Why are things normal in other countries but not here?

Dana. Now, please, Boria.

Boria. Please what? How long will we be there?

Dana. I can't tell you. Nobody knows.

Boria. So, if you don't know, why are you saying it won't be long?

Robinson. Okay, do you have everything? Your thermos, charger . . .

Boria. Come on, let's go!

Dana. Boria, don't shout. Otherwise I'll forget something in the rush.

Boria. You tell me not to shout, but you yell at me! Why do you need a charger now?

Dana. Because if the telephone goes dead we'll have to recharge it.

Boria. But why did you start sticking it in my backpack?

Dana. Because . . .

Boria. Because this is my backpack!

Dana. Boria, stop it, please. You're letting your nerves get to you. You're becoming hysterical. Can we just get ready, and get a grip on ourselves?

Boria. Maybe you're the one getting ready?

Dana. Boria, please, I'm begging you . . .

Boria. Please what?

Robinson. What's funny is that ten years ago, I even had a brief crush on her. But she married another guy, had Boria, then got divorced. In March, Dana suggested I rent a room from her to save both of us money. Now that the war's happened, I deliver drinking water and help her carry things to the shelter and back. In theory, the harsh trials of wartime should bring us together again, so that we finally fall in love for real. But thank God, my personal dramaturgy hasn't gotten that toxic yet. Just the thought of sharing intimacy with her makes me sick. And that pleases me. It means life goes on.

Dana. We'll go there now and play a game . . . But where is my telephone . . .

Boria. You already took it, Mom!

Dana. Dial me, pl . . .

Boria. You already took it! You have it!

Robinson. Here we go. You got everything?

Dana. Robinson, honey, dial my phone, please. I can't find my phone.

Robinson. You just had it in hand.

Dana. Yes, I did, but then I put it somewhere. Oh, here it is.

Robinson. Dana could have become an ideal EU citizen already. She devoutly believes in the values of liberalism, and unquestioningly follows the instructions of the government. As such, when the Kyiv mayor's office announces an air alert, she grabs her son and all her emergency backpacks and races headlong to the bomb shelter. I prefer to stay home, because it is much more comfortable there. And while I help move their things to the shelter, Boria, devastated, casts jealous glances at me. Yes, young man, you are not to be envied. You're at the mercy of your tempestuous mother, who will drag you through stuffy basements full of people. Your position is as shitty as they come, old man.

Dana. Thank you, Robinson honey.

Robinson. We're in touch. You have your charger.

Dana. Yes. If something happens, grab our cat and take him down to the basement.

Robinson. Yes, of course. Here, let me just get a photo of you here in the bomb shelter. To remember the war by, so to speak.

Dana. But we're so disheveled. Oh, all right, okay.

Robinson. Still, a few days later, she found some evacuation bus on the Internet and they hurried off to blessed Poland. So I remain alone in the apartment. Every day the encirclement of Kyiv draws tighter. Yesterday the military airfield in Vasilkovo and the electronic intelligence center in Brovari were knocked out of action. But I'm glad I don't have to pretend to pay attention while Dana reads me another idiotic news item off the Internet with bulging eyes. Moreover, I no longer need to check every time to see if "Boria" peed on the toilet seat. Why hasn't she taught him about that yet?

05.

Robinson. They say that Hollywood's Golden Age began during the Great Depression, when movie theaters were an outlet for suffering Americans. Every day I download an old Woody Allen movie off a torrent tracker. (You can do that now — it's wartime!)

Gill. I'm so happy I ran into you. What are you doing here?

Gabriela. My friends live in this arrondissement. What about you?

Gill. Me? I'm just out walking. But basically, I decided to move to Paris.

Gabriela. You'll like it here.

Gill. Really?

Gabriela. I'm sure you will. You know, I was thinking of you recently. A new Cole Porter record showed up in the store.

Gill. And that made you think about me?

Gabriela. Yes.

Gill. Where are you going now? May I come along?

Gabriela. Yes.

Gill. Oh! It's starting to rain.

Gabriela. No problem. I'm not afraid of getting wet.

Robinson. My God. The actress Léa Seydoux only plays a bit part in this film. But, standing on the banks of the Seine, in a summer dress, with the wind jostling her hair, she is gorgeous. Take it easy, Robinson. Even if it were peacetime now, your chances of meeting a girl like that are negligible. So, life goes on.

Pornhub. Don't despair, dude. Brooke Johnson is back in business. This time, she is subjected to the most delicious torments she has ever experienced. We first see Brooke standing naked in the middle of a dark dungeon. Her sugar daddy uses numerous flexible flogging devices to get things going. Then he lifts her up by the hair on a suspension rig and brings her wet pussy to several hard orgasms. With the aid of a rope he binds her with weighted clamps, stretching her nipples . . .

06.

Father. All right. How about you? Okay?

Robinson. Yeah, I'm okay. There's no big offensive in Kyiv yet. How about Mariupol?

Father. They're shooting.

Robinson. Where are you going to be? At home?

Father. Yes.

Robinson. You got food, everything else?

Father. We're lacking nothing.

Robinson. What do you think? Will it last long?

Father. I don't know. Maybe they'll finish it tomorrow.

Robinson. Uh huh. How are you feeling, Pops?

Father. All right.

Robinson. Okay, tell Mom hello. Let's keep in touch.

Father. Wait a minute.

Robinson. Yeah?

Father. The meter reading . . .

Robinson. What meter?

Father. The gas meter. Write this down — eight hundred, twenty-five cubic meters.

Robinson. Eight hundred twenty-five?

Father. Yeah. That's got to be reported to the Mariupol Gas Company. Online.

Robinson. Yeah, right. I'll pay it. What about electricity?

Father. A little later.

Robinson. Good. Bye-bye then.

07.

Robinson. Voice of America is reporting that Russian troops have approached Kyiv from the west and northwest. British intelligence says the Russian army is approaching from the east and northeast. As I estimate it, I live directly north of the capital. So I guess things aren't so bad. I can still go into the city center. So as not to look suspicious (they're on the constant lookout for saboteurs), I take a grocery bag with me, and put the first book I see into it (not Dostoevsky, God forbid!). There are about five police officers with machine guns at the entrance to the subway. One beckons me to him, and carefully examines my passport. My residence permit is in Mariupol, so I'm a little nervous. *"How long have you been in Kyiv?"* he asks. *"Fifteen years now."* I figure that must be plenty long enough to have undergone cultural assimilation. Apparently, the policeman thinks so, too, and lets me go in.

First, I find myself in a lobby filled with people lying around and sitting on blankets, who, it seems, have decided to wait here for the end of the war. Then I go further down — onto a platform filled with melancholy travelers and their heavy backpacks. The metro is now the Kingdom of Hell. Acheron, the river of sorrow, has ceased to flow. Train cars stand stationary on it so people may rest in them. The train runs only to Styx. In intervals of one hour. Satisfied with my uncomplicated metaphor, I assume the familiar pose of an inner snob. "Each of these people was here on an important matter. While I, as always, am an accidental guest," I think, condescendingly looking at my fellow travelers. Suddenly I remember they have been bombing Mariupol for two weeks now, and there is no electricity, water, food, or medicine there. And that Father hasn't been in touch all this time. I even close my eyes because I'm afraid I might see him and Mother here. But then I smile. Because parents are immortal gods, with whom everything will always be all right.

JFr

Commissioned by a grant from Philip Arnoult's Center
for International Theatre Development

OUR CHILDREN
NATALIA BLOK

My family today is in occupied Kherson. My dad, my uncle, my sister, and my three children. Matvei is the eldest. The youngest are Herman and Tikhon.

Kherson was occupied by the fascist Russians on the first day of the war. Battles came to us by way of Crimea. Battles came to us from Mykolaiv. Tanks crossed the Antonivskiy Bridge and the first rockets and bombs hit the suburbs of Kherson. The Ruscists took Oleshki, Kakhovka, and the village of Tiaginka where my youngest, Tikhon, was born, and they seized the city of Kherson.

Two weeks before that my ex-husband had written to me. He asked for permission to take our children abroad. Like all of us, he feared Russia's military build-up on the Ukrainian border. We talked about that, and I found out that permission was not necessary. His plan was to go to Poland, then the Czech Republic, by car. Aside from my youngest boys, he would go with his wife and their five-year-old son Lukas.

I called Herman, who had just turned 13 in January, a month before bombs began falling all over Ukraine. I asked if they had left yet. Herman said that Lukas woke him at 5 a.m. and told him to pack his things, they were getting ready to go. They spent a lot of time and energy getting ready . . . In short, I don't know what went wrong, and I'm not going to ask, but the boys' father decided it was too dangerous to go, so they stayed home.

That was a very bad decision. A very, very bad decision. All these days I keep wondering why he made that decision. Because on that first day it was still possible to leave by car. My friend Maryna got her son out to Uzhgorod. She had a car. Trains that day were not coming to Kherson.

My eldest, Matvei, who lives with his aunt, my sister, was also in Kherson. That day he called several times and gave me some good advice. *"Mom, grab all your valuables, documents, and money in a sack, and carry it with you at all times. If you go out without a backpack, when they bomb the house you'll have no documents."* He wasn't planning on leaving. Because he was liable to be mobilized because of his age. He was very happy. He said the explosions were far away from him. He didn't hear any sirens in his area. The basement in their building had been fixed up. He had already sealed up the windows. Okay. I'm very happy that his character is so easy-going. And that he has matured so that he can give me such excellent advice. I know that his friends from Donbas were probably the ones who advised him.

It's hellish horrible to think about advice like that. Why should our children have knowledge like this?

Sirens howled all the time in Kyiv where I was at that time. The basement was horrible and they were killing people wherever they could. I stood in line for medicine and called my friend Dima. Dima was in a positive frame of mind, too. He said he'd been waiting for war a long time, and that Ukraine would win, that Russia had signed its own death warrant, and would fall apart in a few years, and that he had food for the next two months, and he would share with Matvei. That made me feel better.

Not for long, though. Maybe it was that same day when I acquired the habit of checking to see if Matvei was online, or if my younger sons were online.

Matvei wrote that his aunt was very worried, but he was not. He heard several explosions and the house shook. He wrote that the basement was a good place to be. Although it's bad that there's only one exit. Still, he thinks they'll dig him out if something happens. He wrote this as if it wasn't the first war in his life, but the thirty-first.

I constantly watched the news and saw that tanks were headed for Kherson. I called my youngest son, my ten-year-old Tikhon. He calmly said he could hear explosions. I asked if he was scared. He said, *"Why should I be scared?"*

How good it is that he doesn't know that one should fear explosions. How I would love it if he never had to learn that.

That evening they wrote on the Internet that the Russians were trying to seize the Chernobyl atomic station. I wrote about that to Matvei. My son said there was no radiation there and that he was going to bed.

I thought: It's so good he is so positive and carefree, and that he can sleep.

But it's not all that simple. The next night Matvei wrote me that the news was saying Kyiv would be bombed at 3 a.m., and that I should go down to the basement. And that he had heard lots of explosions, but they were far away, so he wasn't going to go to the basement. I did, though. Because the siren howled and the explosions were nearby.

The next day, after a sleepless night in the basement, I telephoned my children but couldn't get through. Not to any of them. I called their father. He didn't answer either. I began to worry and I decided to wait out the next siren in the bathroom.

Just as I called my children, my mother called from abroad. I got the impression she was more worried than I was.

I called my children again. I wrote to them on Messenger. In fact Tikhon is on Viber, Matvei's on Telegram, and Herman uses Discord. Three sons — three different worlds. I wrote them, but they didn't answer. All messengers were silent.

Finally I reached their father.

He was calm and said they had a good basement in their building. All was good. He would put the kids in the car and get them out of town at the first opportunity. That calmed me down some. No one knew then that no such opportunity would arise soon, and that there would be only death and rockets.

Matvei wrote that he decided to stock up on cigarettes. My sister did the same with food. They would wait out the end of the war, and he had already seen two people with machine guns.

The next day I left Kyiv and sat in a traffic jam without internet for twelve hours. When I finally got internet, I saw Matvei had written to say he was worried, and that our Ukrainian heroes were dying here and now. And that he believed our army would defeat the Orcs.

Tikhon and Herman slept that night in the bomb shelter. I didn't sleep at all that night because I was in my car on the road.

Tikhon said after that night he was feeling good. And that, in general, he was quite happy now. I asked, what are you so happy about? He said, because I'm still alive. He said that in a weak voice, a voice I would never want to hear my son speak in.

My 13-year-old Herman was very depressed. He said Putin would win because there are 140 million of them and 30 million of us. He always loved math, and he studied in a special math class that he had really wanted to join.

Mathematics is a fine science, but we are defending our land. I wanted to believe Matvei.

He told me the news. The Russians were planning on deporting Ukrainians from Kherson. They would throw them in police vans and take them somewhere. They had found 1,000 Ukrainian military uniforms and they would change into them and would lead people out of the city disguised as Ukrainians. Then Matvei added optimistically that that's all not so important, and that the main thing now was not to open doors for the Russians.

I called Matvei again when I was in a day-long line on the border. There was no internet, but my phone worked. Matvei said that the Russians had bombed the only entertainment center in town, the water canal, killed 30 young men from territorial defense, and that his friend sent a video showing the bodies of Khersonians blown to pieces.

The youngest boys disappeared again. I had no communication with them. I was very worried. I imagined the horrible picture of a bomb landing on their building.

Basically, my body was who-knows-where, but in my thoughts I was always in Kherson. I read all the news about Kherson. Some was fake. Some was real. The worst news was not about the shelling, but about the fact that food had disappeared from stores, medicines from pharmacies, and that the women of Kherson were giving birth in basements.

Basically, there was a very optimistic video from the chief doctor of a maternity ward. He taped it in the basement of a maternity ward and there were lots of women around him. He said almost everyone had given birth, and that just a few were left. The women tried to smile.

Meanwhile, the Russian occupants wandered around the city shooting up whatever they wanted, robbing stores, and killing people. The telephone and internet in Kherson were constantly cutting out. But I read that and tried not to worry. My friend from Kherson wrote that the Russians had killed the son of his teacher in Kherson.

All news of that kind, all such reports, made me look at my phone and check all the messengers of my three sons. In order. Viber: "Tikhon was last seen online 4 hours ago." Okay, he'd been in contact. Discord: Herman changed his status. "I make avatars on commission. Russia is bombing my place of residence. So I often sit in a bomb shelter with no internet."

Matvei – Telegram: "Last seen online yesterday."

Yesterday was a nervous day. I called my sister to hear her say that everyone was okay, that everyone was alive, and that there was plenty of food.

I reached a temporary shelter for Ukrainians. There were mothers with their children. The children asked questions like, *"Why is Putin bombing us? That's not fair, Mom. His country is bigger. What does he want from us? Why are they killing us? Is the sky closed over us here in Poland? Why don't they close the sky over Ukraine? What is that sound?"*

Children showed me pictures of them sitting in basements, and they told me how important it was to hide when the sirens blow. They told about the dog they left with a neighbor because they couldn't take it with them. Children and adults all shuddered whenever there were loud sounds. The mothers of the children told how their men, to the very last, were defending Ukraine with arms in hand.

A few days later Herman made me a new avatar against the background of a Ukrainian flag, and said he was going to organize a quest.

Matvei photoshopped some memes about "Hate Russia."

Tikhon simply said everything was okay and that he loved me.

The invaders in Kherson seized the local jail. I think it's so it will remind them of the prison they live in at home.

People in Kherson were going out to protest. I posted a photo on Facebook of one such rally. It showed a girl holding a poster with the words "Putin has a small dick."

The Russian Nazis shot up a car filled with children near Kakhovka. There was no green corridor. All my children remained in Kherson. The shops were closed or empty. Although sometimes you could buy food. My children assured me that they had plenty of food. And I cooked soup, thinking that maybe they have nothing to eat. And that hunger was coming. My stomach clenched, and my hands began to shake.

Ukraine sent 16 vehicles with humanitarian aid to Kherson.

The occupiers would not let them into the city. They set up their own food centers in Kherson's main square. And do you know what the people of Kherson did? They just didn't come. They would not come for that Russky food.

Instead, they went out to protest again. I saw a video where shots were fired, and city residents shouted *"Shame"* at them. One guy with a big flag of Ukraine climbed on a Russky tank and waved his flag. And the tank drove away.

That calmed me a bit. I thought maybe people weren't so hungry there. But my animal, maternal fear, and my desire to feed my children, almost made it impossible for me to breathe.

Yesterday Matvei told me how to write about where he is now. He had started working on a different project. This morning I talked to Herman. He said Kherson is quiet, the bombs here are coming from Mykolaiv, and that, if they were to leave, they would go to Spain because some relatives of their father had found an apartment there. I thought, they can go wherever they want, as long as there is no war there. But it still wasn't possible to leave.

Herman joked that grandma was going to inflate a rubber boat and they would sail it down the Dnipro River to the Canary Islands that night. Such a sad little joke.

Herman also said he loves me very much. And I love him very much, and Tikhon, and Matvei, and my sister, and Kherson, and all Ukrainians.

For many days now I have wanted to hear that my children are safe. I probably never wanted anything so much in my life. My head is full of chaos, fuck-knows-what, and my Kherson. And all of our children.

JFr & NB

Commissioned by a grant from Philip Arnoult's Center for International Theatre Development

TDP
[TEMPORARILY DISPLACED PERSONS]
KATERYNA PENKOVA

I find accommodations for temporarily displaced persons.

For those who have been left homeless.
I place them in Warsaw and Kyiv.
In my hostels.
More precisely, in premises that were hostels before the war.
They're not mine. They are all rented.

FIRST. Good afternoon. I wanted to ask you. We are from Mariupol. There are two of us. My son and I. He is 15. We will be in Kyiv on Thursday. We must go to the prosecutor general's office to present our son's DNA samples. His mother is missing. May we stay in your hostel for a few days?

SECOND. I need a place for one young man. He is from the Kharkiv region. His leg was broken by incoming rocketfire at the Ministry of Defense. He will be released tomorrow from hospital No. 17. He's still on crutches. First floor if possible.

THIRD. Hello, we are making a hasty departure from occupied territory (Zaporizhzhia region, Vasylivka district): a family of four (mom, dad, and two children), plus three cats and a Chihuahua (well-mannered, strictly potty-trained to go only in a litter box). Is it possible for us to stay in your hostel for a short time?

FOURTH. Good afternoon. We need a room for five people tomorrow — mom, dad, and children.

FIFTH. Good afternoon. Be so kind as to tell me, is there a place where you can shelter a family from Kramatorsk?

SIXTH. Hello, I was given your contact information. They said you can provide temporary housing. Please help me. I myself am from the Luhansk region, village of Rubizhne. Our house was destroyed because of the war. My child and I are now in Kyiv. I'm sorry to bother you.

SEVENTH. Good evening. Tell me, please, do you provide temporary housing for refugees? My son and I are in the city of Kyiv and have been living at the train station for two nights. Can you take us, even if separately, but at least somewhere, for a couple of days?

The hostel is located near the train station.
You can. I'll take you if I can.
I receive 30 such messages every day via Viber, Telegram, and Messenger.
And about 30 more direct calls from Ukraine, although I always encourage people to text me via instant messengers.
I feel terrible when I have no place to put them, but they keep calling and calling and calling . . .
Tomorrow my parents will be leaving Kyiv.
My father had a stroke and practically cannot walk.

TDP [Temporarily Displaced Persons]

My mother has a bad back.
We have no relatives left in Kyiv.
Their son, my brother, died in April.
I had just one request for everyone presently living in the hostel — to help my parents catch the train . . .
And not one person stepped up to make themselves useful . . .
Maybe it's because I am still paying off some debt . . .
Or because I myself am not so helpless . . .
Or because they themselves are in such confusion . . .
Or maybe they are struggling with money problems . . .
Or . . . I don't know why.

JFr & NB

Commissioned by a grant from Philip Arnoult's Center
for International Theatre Development

MY TARA
LIUDMYLA TYMOSHENKO

There is a scene in *Gone with the Wind,* the funeral of Gerald, Scarlett's father. Before closing the coffin, Will asks Scarlett to go into the house, saying she is pregnant and might lose her child in the heat. The old woman accompanying her says, "He just didn't want you to hear the coffin being nailed shut. And he's right. Remember, Scarlett: until you hear that sound, the person seems alive to you. But as soon as you hear . . . Yes, it is the most frightening sound in the world. It is the sound of the end."

I was twelve years old when I read these lines. At that time I lived with my grandmother Tania in Ovruch in the Zhytomyr region of Ukraine. When I was seven months old, my parents had sent me from North Kazakhstan, which is where I was born, to live with her. My father served in the Strategic Rocket Forces. What does that mean? When rockets were placed on combat duty, they had to be kept under constant control. They were guided via underground command posts, and they were called "Satan's warheads"—the largest nuclear rockets of the time. (There were 24 of them in my dad's garrison.) Officers sat underground keeping constant watch over these rockets. Every officer on duty knew if he were to receive the order, he would have to press a button.

There were three types of readiness. Number One was "constant combat readiness," whereby a green signal light was constantly on in the bunker. Number Two was "increased combat readiness," which was accompanied by a blue light. The third was "engagement danger." For this a red light was lit, and the officer on duty would turn on all devices that eventually would direct the warheads toward their target. All that was left was to push the red button. The officer on duty knew that by pushing that button, he could destroy a city ten times the size of Hiroshima and Nagasaki combined.

I was sent from North Kazakhstan to live with my grandmother in Ukraine because the climate in Kazakhstan is not suitable for a seven-month-old child. Ten months of winter and the rest is summer, as the locals joked. Forty-below in winter, plus-forty in summer. I was often ill. My older brother Serhiy stayed with our parents. He, a five-year-old boy, was very scared. Like all Soviet children living in such military bases, he feared nuclear war. At the age of five, he knew perfectly well what "unauthorized behavior" was. This topic was constantly discussed among parents, kindergarten teachers, neighbors, shop assistants, and even hairdressers in beauty shops. The officers on duty were usually men of strong endurance and iron-clad psyche. From time to time, however, their nerves might crack. The nerves they experienced in the control room staring at the color of the signal light made some of them go crazy. Mental aberrations like this had to be detected or foreseen in some way. Otherwise, this so-called "unauthorized behavior" might actually transpire. That is, if a duty officer realized he had the power to flatten Planet Earth all on his own, he might succumb to the notion he could do anything he pleased.

Such "system failures" might occur not only in a particular person's head, but also in the bunker's control system. There once was an incident when something went haywire and the red signal light came on completely by accident. While the officer on duty, sweating with animal terror, aimed the rocket at its target, the command center managed to issue the proper directives to rescind the order.

I was not afraid of nuclear war because I lived with my grandmother. She ate dumplings with cherries in summer, and mashed potatoes with gravy in winter. My grandmother took me sledding, drove me to see the New Year's tree, and every Victory Day on May 9, we would attend the parade of flags, rejoicing at the peaceful sky over our heads, and our victory over fascism. My grandfather died in 1958. During World War II, he fought on various fronts, repairing military aircraft. He met my grandmother in Germany where, like many girls, she had been transported by train from Ukraine, and forced to work in German factories. After the war, my grandmother and grandfather, along with my father's newborn older brother Valeriy (named after test pilot Valeriy Chkalov), moved to a garrison in Belarus in the city of Baranavichy. When my dad Viktor was 9 years old, his father died. Over the Easter holidays Grandpa went from Belarus to his native village in the Zhytomyr region and got caught up in the tradition of going "house to house" (this is when, on holidays, from morning to night, villagers visit their neighbors and drink moonshine). He then returned to his family in Baranovychi and died of a stroke. He so missed my grandmother that, immediately upon arrival, he climbed up on top of her and his heart burst. He was 38 years old. My grandmother, my father, and his brother Valeriy remember the sounds of the nails being driven into the coffin. Eight months after grandfather's death, grandmother decided to return to her relatives in Ukraine. She and her two sons were given a room in a communal house in the town of Ovruch. Grandfather's family asked for permission to transport his body to his native village near Ovruch, and, to make this happen, Grandma sold her last valuable possession, a war trophy, a German accordion captured during the war. The coffin was dug up, covered with fir branches to hide the smell of the corpse, and reburied in Grandpa's hometown cemetery. To this day Dad can't stand the smell of pine needles. Then my grandmother was given the house where I had come to live from North Kazakhstan when I was seven months old, and where I lived until I was eight, at which time my parents took me to Lviv.

This red brick house was the happiest place I've ever known. On every school holiday, I "flew" there on wings. (Actually, I traveled by way of the Lviv-Luhansk railway with a train change in Korosten.) I've always strongly associated the smell of the jasmine growing near the house with the beginning of everlasting happiness. School would end on May 25, and on May 26 I would luxuriate in the smell of the white flowers from this bush. There would be three months of wonderful carefree time ahead of me.

That summer I received a two-volume edition of *Gone with the Wind* as a gift. This book was in short supply, and to get it you had to turn in more than 20 kilos of wastepaper. I imagined myself as Scarlett O'Hara, and I saw my grandmother's house as Tara. A whole new wonderful world opened up for me. The parts about the war bored me, but I reread the parts about Scarlett and Rhett many times over. When I read those lines about the sounds of the end, I was frightened for the first time in my life. I realized that one day my grandmother would die, and I would hear those sounds. Fortunately, that didn't happen until I was 40. My grandmother outlived her husband by 53 years, and when she was buried in the family cemetery in the village, the locals said they still remembered Grandpa's coffin which had been covered with fir branches. Grandma died at the age of 92. The women who dressed her in her funeral gown tied up her opened lower jaw with a handkerchief. They pulled the knot so hard that Grandma smiled in her coffin. I was prepared for the sounds of the nails going into the coffin.

I was not ready for the sounds of rockets flying over Kyiv at 5 a.m. on February 24. I was not ready for the sound of the air raid siren outside the window of my Kyiv apartment. I was not ready for my mother to spend eight days under fire in occupied Irpin without water, gas, electricity, or mobile communications until she was evacuated. Most of all I was not ready for several shells to explode 300 meters from my grandmother's house in Ovruch, where my father Viktor now lives. Our neighbors' houses were completely destroyed, and the roof of my childhood home was partly blown off, while all the windows were blown out. Dad called me and said, *"Liuda, listen to this sound."* It was the sound of my Tara's windows being hammered shut with boards and plywood. It was the true sound of the end, for which I was not prepared.

I was not afraid at the age of five, but I now am afraid of nuclear war. Because the president of Russia, the country that attacked my Ukraine, shows all signs of that "unauthorized behavior." I am afraid of falling asleep and never waking up. My brother Serhiy, who is currently a surgeon on 24-hour duty at a hospital in Kyiv, told me: *"In North Kazakhstan, every adult and child knew what 'Dead Hand' was."* That was a system that could launch rockets at the enemy without human intervention, even if a nuclear strike in our direction had been inflicted earlier. As such there was nothing to fear. But fuck knows if anything can stop it.

P.S. My dad's brother, my uncle Valeriy, named after the great test pilot Valeriy Chkalov, now lives in Bryansk, in Russia. He and his family consider us fascists and they support the Russian president in this war.

10 March 2022

JFr & NB

Commissioned by a grant from Philip Arnoult's Center
for International Theatre Development

I WANT TO GO HOME

OKSANA SAVCHENKO

It's very difficult for me to catch the rhythm. Very difficult to catch the rhythm. Hatred is the only thing that hardens me. When I look at a photo of the bombed maternity ward in Mariupol, hatred blossoms in my heart. For the Ruscists. My colleague can't find her parents. They lived in Mariupol. I tell my colleague she should leave Kyiv and go abroad, but I get a clear answer — *"I will go nowhere without my parents. I will go nowhere without my parents. Either we will get out together. Or we die together."*

Hatred is born in my heart when I read comments under the posts of fashionable Ruscist bloggers, like "What have we done?" Hatred and anger are purely physiological sensations. War and physiology go hand in hand, shoulder to shoulder, like Siamese twins. This cannot be explained, just as childbirth cannot be explained. Hatred makes it difficult to breathe. It's hard to breathe. Hatred makes you want to kill. You want to kill the one who kills you. When I fled my hometown, I took a knife. I took a knife to protect my child. My child is not afraid of air raid sirens. She is no longer afraid of air raid sirens. When we first fled to a bomb shelter, my daughter was frightened and said odd, scary things like *"I had plans for life, I don't want to die. I had plans."* My child is 12 years old. We all had plans for life. Now the ground has been pulled out from under my feet. I have no plans. I stand strong only because I love those who remain at home.

Since the war began, my eyesight has been shot. I never wore glasses. At school, I teased all the four-eyes. Now I've received my comeuppance. I can't see letters without glasses. Although vision does return when your child is in danger. When your child is in mortal danger. You can read even the tiniest letters in a screenshot if the text concerns your child's safety. And you grow strong standing on the step of a train, pulling your child from a crowd. From a crowd of mad people shouting, *"Please! Please!"* at the conductress. You pull your child out of the crowd by her arm. Your child's wearing a funny hat with a pompom on top. Very touching. And you are very strong at this moment, pulling your child, who is on the step of the train, by her arm.

As a teenager, I dreamed of my school lifting off into the sky. This was school No.153, named after Pushkin in Kyiv. Now bombs are falling there. You must be careful what you wish for. You never know when your wish will come true. My school named after Pushkin, which no one ever thought of renaming until the Russian whores began bombing Ukraine. Until the Russian Orcs began bombing Kyiv. I hope my school will be renamed. I will be the first to create a petition. I will make sure that no school in Ukraine ever again bears the name of a Russian poet or writer.

The OHMATDET Children's Hospital stands across the street from my school. The OHMATDET Children's Hospital where sick children are brought from all over Ukraine. Sick children whose kidneys do not function, who need dialysis. Sick children with cancer. Children sick with poisoning and fractures are brought here too. There is no one there but children and doctors. I know because in peacetime I did a report on OHMATDET. There are no strategic facilities there. Nothing but my school No.153, named after Pushkin. As a result of the first shelling, one child who was being treated at OHMATDET died. I know that for a fact. I don't know how many are dead now.

Since the war began, my eyesight has been shot. I can't see letters without glasses. My eyesight came back only once — when I was able to read an important message in a screenshot. It was a life and death message. Your vision sharpens when it comes to life and death. Hatred is a physiological property. I write in Russian and I hate it. I write in Russian — because I want this text to be read by Russians. I realized that hatred is a purely physiological feeling when I was at a cold train station, and I watched a crowd of people get off the train with their dogs. The train spat people out onto the snow-covered platform as my child does chewing gum. Chewing gum. The chewing gum is bloody because my child's nose is bleeding. Blood flows. Although my child is calm. There is blood coming from her nose. This is how anxiety manifests itself. The anxiety that my little girl has been trying to contain all this time. The fact that the passengers arrived from Kyiv could be read on their faces. It's easy to read faces when everyone has one face. War puts a stamp on faces. A singular stamp. You can read us by the circles under our eyes. We all have circles under our eyes now. Circles under the eyes are a sign of war. The stamp of war.

What's most difficult is seeing old people in wheelchairs being dragged along muddy tire tracks (I forgot how to say that in Russian). Their relatives drag them over these ruts. They drag children too. On leashes they drag huge breeds of dogs with short tails. Naturally, some child carries a teddy bear. A bowlegged bear rumbles through the woods. And now a Russian bear stalks my land with its damned, ugly paws. This bear has the frightened face of a conscript who has shit his pants out of fear. His name is "fodder." I do not feel sorry for conscripts. Shit on them. I do not feel sorry for Russian soldiers. Shit on them. I do not feel sorry for Russian women who will not be able to buy up IKEA. IKEA? They won't be able to buy it up. Burn in hell, bitches.

I feel sorry for our Ukrainian children, our elderly, and our women who tried to escape the war but were killed by the Russian occupiers. The photos are on the Internet. Right there on the Internet. This evidence of the crimes of Russian soldiers will resurface in The Hague.

In the meantime, horses. There once lived a horse near Kyiv. She lived in a good stable. She was four years old. For a horse, four is the age of a teenager. Translated into a human age, it's about 12 years or so. Like my daughter. The horse's name was Frailey — a horse receives its name by way of its parents — part of the father's name and part of the mother's name. Thus one arrives at a horse's name. Frailey. A pinto. A Ukrainian horse breed.

A beautiful horse that my daughter rode. My daughter. A small tragedy occurred near Kyiv, revealing the special cruelty of those Russian whores, those stinking, stupid Orcs. They seized the stable where my child used to go. They brutalized the stableman on the third or fourth day of the war. The beginning of the war. They made the stableman crawl face-down, flat on the ground. Crawl to a marked limit in two minutes' time. Otherwise he would be shot. To crawl over earth dusted with snow. Otherwise he would be shot. The stableman went into the stables to feed the horses. To feed horses who compete in competitions. Show jumping and dressage. Good horses that have never been offended by humans. Then, there was Nick's dog — small and smiling. The whores took over the stables. The whores don't know what to feed horses. Horses who had never experienced cruelty. One little pony named Coquette always smiled at me. The Russians captured the stables and starved the horses. Starved them. One man tried to reach the horses to feed them, but he was killed by the Russian beasts. Killed. Russian whores kill people. Does it make sense to talk about starving horses when Russian Orcs are killing civilians in Ukraine? Does it make sense to talk about Frailey, who is four years old — that's about 12 human years? Does it make sense to talk about a horse? When children are dying? Does it make sense to talk about a pony I always loved when children are dying? Does it make sense to talk about horses when people are dying? When children are dying? When children are dying of dehydration? We're not talking about Frailey. We don't know what's happened to her. We keep hoping. We know that one good little pony is dead. We know that five more horses are dead. No, we're not talking about Frailey.

[*Voice switches into Ukrainian. She speaks only in Ukrainian from here to the end of the monologue. The actor might remind an audience of that from time to time*. Translator's note.]

I call my mom and say *"povitria,"* "air," in Ukrainian. I call my father and say *"povitria,"* "air," in Ukrainian. I call Sasha and say *"povitria,"* "air," in Ukrainian. I hear their tired, calm voices. And I am ashamed to be here, while they are there in Kyiv. In Ukrainian my father says: *"Daughter, you never let us sleep all your childhood, you never let us sleep. Now that you're an adult, shhh, let us sleep. We are okay. We are okay."* They are in a large apartment building with a few other elderly people. I can't breathe because of my hatred for the Russian whores. I can't breathe.

War is when you can't breathe. Out of hatred. War is when your body is convulsed with pain out of fear for your relatives. It is when you escape abroad with your child and spend all your time scrolling through the news. When you can't admire the sights of Europe's beautiful streets. Your heart is at home. You live at home. You learn what to do in the event there is a chemical attack on your family. You run to them. You cry. You can't cry. It was easier in Kyiv. It was easier on your own home ground. You are ashamed that you left.

You live only by the news and chats with your friends. Your legs are weak. Your relatives from Kyiv are hanging on. You're sort of hanging on, and you don't cry. You are safe, damn it. Although after what happened, you know there are no safe places. Everything can change in one day.

At first you try to pressure your relatives — it's time to get you out of Kyiv, what are you thinking? You make recommendations, because you yourself already left. But then mother says in a low voice that she doesn't have a small suitcase. She does not have a small suitcase, and in her intonation you feel the beating of her heart. She's afraid. She's glad you got out, you bitch, but she's there, there with Dad, two defenseless people remaining in a high-rise building with a handful of neighbors. And you decide to shut up. You decide to shut up, because any pressure from those who abandoned those who remained is like beating a defenseless little child. It's like beating a child.

I had a girlfriend. We went to Crimea together. My friend's name was Ira Dubrova. We went to Crimea back in the first decade of the century, when our biggest problem was finding the meaning of life, and pants that fit our butts. My friend lived in Bucha, a small town near Kyiv. My friend was last online on March 2. March 2. She has been out of touch. Out of touch. Her mother has diabetes. There are problems with insulin in Kyiv. Bucha was blown to bits. I try to imagine my friend and her mother hiding in a basement. As she rescues her cat. I try to find her, I send inquiries. No one knows anything. I look back over our text messages. I remember how we walked around Crimea in the early years of the 2000s, how we drank wine, how we got sick to our stomachs, how we listened to music. I remember when our biggest question was why in hell are we alive? Not how do we survive. I hope my girlfriend is alive. Maybe she just dropped her phone when she was boarding an evacuation bus. Just dropped her phone.

Evening. Curfew in Kyiv. I call the man I love. We talk about the day. Talk about how the day went. Softly, with my hand, I caress the screen where his cheek is. I want to kiss him but I can't. There is distance between us. There is a war between us. And I want him so much.

I so want to be with him.

I want to go home.

12 March 2022

JFr & NB

Commissioned by a grant from Philip Arnoult's Center for International Theatre Development

DIARY OF SURVIVAL OF A CIVILIAN URBANITE IN CONDITIONS OF WAR
PAVLO ARIE

For Birgit

A year ago, I lost a relationship with the person I loved — and still love — more than anything. Throughout this year, I've done nothing but let myself suffer and complain about my health. It was a long, drawn-out depression. Every day I said to myself, "I'm tired. I've lost the meaning of life. I'm in a stupor. I do not know what to write about, what to make performances about. I do not know what to think about." In January this year, I realized I needed the help of a therapist. I should have done it long ago, but I avoided it under any and all pretexts. Subconsciously I wanted to destroy myself. I finally took the plunge and got in touch via Zoom with a female psychotherapist. Her name is Dina. She is wonderful. She had helped many of my friends. But my attempt to help myself was a fiasco. We only met in Zoom three times, and each of our conversations had dubious and painful consequences for me. On the physical level, I began to feel unbearable pains in my stomach, from which I could not sleep, sit, or lie down. I went to the hospital to see a gastroenterologist. They examined me but found nothing. They said my pain and infernal constipation were attacking me by way of my head. They prescribed antidepressants, painkillers, a strict diet, and advised me to stop working with a psychotherapist. That kind of thing happens too. But my psychotherapeutic Dina left me one beautiful thing that I use every day. She advised me to keep a diary of my feelings, and I downloaded a special app to my phone. It helps you achieve a sense of yourself, draw conclusions every day, respect your feelings, and be aware of them. Thus did the idea of a diary come to me, and when the war began it intensified. I realized the diary was my salvation, it was my attempt to be useful to myself. On the second day of the war, I began randomly recording everything that was important to me, my thoughts, my actions . . . I began recording the world around me, as I saw it, all the changes. It helped me invent my own ways not to go completely mad, to pull myself together and calm down. A few days ago, in a conversation with my colleague and close friend Birgit Legens, I mentioned I was saving myself by writing a diary. Birgit asked if my diary might be useful to others, but I didn't have an answer to her question. I did realize, however, that this diary of mine might help people from other places, places where there is no war, places where war has long been forgotten, to understand what is going on. To let them hear from people for whom war, in one day, in one instant, became a reality. To see how war exposes a person, tears off the social masks that we wear so skillfully in normal ritualized life, turns inside out the best, and even the most bitter of its qualities. I allow myself to be as subjective as possible in this diary. These are my thoughts, my actions, my assessments. They are not necessarily correct. Some people will be very offended by what I write here. I realize I am wrong in many ways, but this is how I feel and I want to be frank. My diary is the action of a person who cannot, does not want to, pick up a machine gun or a Molotov cocktail.

WAR. DAY ONE
24 February 2022

For me, this full-scale war begins with the word "war." I wake up to explosion-like sounds. The first thing I see is the glowing screen of my mobile phone. The screen says, "Mom."

My mother's voice says, *"war."*

My mother tells me to get ready to come to her, to Lviv, a city in western Ukraine that is considered the safest because it is far from Russia, or to go to Germany. I have a permanent residence permit there. I lived in Germany for 16 years, but now I have been working in a theater in Kyiv for two years. After finishing our conversation, I start looking for train tickets to Lviv. Everything is sold out for the next few days, and the site constantly crashes. Obviously there are thousands of people like me at this moment. I think: "Damn, the war is increasingly growing nearer to Kyiv." More explosions, real and close, shaking windows, the smell of burning on the street. I don't believe it yet, this can't happen to us in 2022. I write a post on FB:

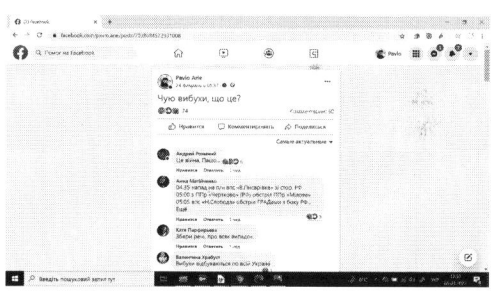

Photo 1.*

*The post asks: "I hear explosions. What is that?"

Maybe it's just a mistake. Maybe there is another explanation. The war in Donbas is hundreds of kilometers away. This is Kyiv, the center of Europe. In responses from friends on Facebook, and in apocalyptic news reports with the volume turned up full-blast, life is divided into "before" and "now." In my backpack, I pack my documents, a pair of underpants, a pair of socks, a T-shirt, an apple, water, antidepressants, sedatives, and painkillers. I start thinking feverishly about how to leave and how to calm my mother down. Calls, chats, news from all channels at the same time, running from room to room, emptying the contents of cabinets out on the floor, repeating the same actions in circles. For a moment, I realize I will go mad if I don't stop scrambling around. I turn everything off, turn off the sound in my phone, and I immediately want to sleep. This is my typical reaction to severe stress.

Sleep is the best thing I can do.

When I wake up several hours later, I explain to my mother that I couldn't leave today, and that this is very good for me.

I realize that I do not feel fear, but rather concern for my family, friends, acquaintances, for my theater, for Ukraine. In a purely human sense, this is a very important realization for me, because I realize that most people feel the same way.

The news says we are holding strong, the world is behind us, and weapons are being distributed to everyone in Kyiv. It is enough for us just to have a passport, now, just like in Switzerland, and we'll all have weapons. Wow! Fuck Putin. La, la, la.

I down some sedatives and I am knocked out until nightfall. That evening, my mother calls from Lviv during an air raid alarm. They are going to hide in an underground garage ten minutes from her house. They have transferred food and water underground. The night is sleepless as I search for all possible news. Cruise missiles explode all across the country. It's dangerous everywhere. The awareness of a new reality arises — yesterday I lived in a different, safe world, but everything changed in an instant.

DAY TWO
25 February 2022

Seven a.m., a call from Mother, everyone is alive.
Many messages and emails from friends from all corners of the world: Germany, Japan, England, USA, France, Venezuela, Chile, Georgia, Poland, Israel, Lebanon, and none from Russia. I have a lot of friends there. Many are even relatives. People that I haven't spoken to in 20 years have remembered me. Thank you!

I write a response on Facebook to everyone: "I'm alive!"

Many of those with cars grabbed children, parents, dogs and cats, and went to Lviv, or to the border. Only women, children, and men over the age of 60 are allowed to leave Ukraine. As such, men take their people to the border and stay — some in the cities of western Ukraine, some return to Kyiv, Kharkiv, Kherson, and Mykolaiv to take up arms and defend the country.

In Kyiv, air raid alerts follow one after another, the city is moving to bomb shelters and underground metro stations. Women and children and those who are able to get tickets are put on evacuation trains. People ride standing up for 10 to 20 hours.

My friend, the actor Oleh Stefan, who also lives on the left bank of Kyiv, got a train ticket for tomorrow, and he encourages me to break through to the station with him, and to leave together on his single seat. I can't imagine how I can push through to the train, competing with women holding children in their arms. I refuse. I reassure my mother. I say I will come if someone takes me in a car with them.

I go to the pharmacy to pick up blood pressure medication that I ordered. My blood pressure sometimes jumps when I'm very nervous, and I'm nervous now. My pharmacy, like everything else in my area, is closed. Desperate people approach pharmacies then keep on searching.

Only grocery stores are open. There are incredible lines in front of them. I need to buy something to eat, so I get in line. The adults are very quiet, thoughtful, and anxious. Everyone understands this is just the beginning. But the children who came with them — and there are a lot of them — are excited. The children are having fun. For children this is a genuine adventure. An air raid alert sounds, most people disperse and go to the bomb shelters. I do, too.

The bomb shelter nearest to my home is eight minutes away. The alarm has been canceled. I don't go to the store, I just go home.

Another alarm, explosions are heard. I meet a neighbor-woman on the stairs with a 6-year-old daughter and teenage son, and we go to the shelter together. We decide to stay in the vault all night because running back and forth is not an option. A terrible night, in the cold, sitting and lying on the floor. Children crying, people walking around. I feel very sorry for myself, but even more sorry for all these grandmothers, mothers, children, dads, grandfathers, frightened cats in carriers, and dogs. I am young and strong, and alone. (I answer only for myself.) If it is very difficult for me, how difficult must it be for all of them?

My mother calls every half hour. She is very worried. She begs me to come to them. It's safer there. We'll all be together there.

At midnight, they also have an alarm in Lviv. They will spend the night in a garage that stinks of cars and gasoline. Fuck!

I ask: *"Mom, send a photo of how things are there. I want to see."*

The expressions on the faces of my relatives shock me. I barely recognize them. I sit quietly crying. Mom, I'll be there. Mom, I'll be with you soon! I'm sorry it took me so long. Tomorrow I will write a post about them. Let everyone see these faces.

My Facebook post: "This is my mother and her husband. Mom is 76 years old. Today, because of the air raid, she will spend the night in an underground garage in an old car. Mom is in Lviv.

DAY THREE
26 February 2022

I get home at 6 a.m., more tired than ever, my body aching from the uncomfortable hard surfaces in the shelter. My head is splitting, my blood pressure is leaping, and I'm taking my last pill. This is fucked up. What should I do?

I talk on the phone with my mother. Everyone is alive but very tired.

Photo 2.

I have only one thing in my head: I want to sleep! I haven't slept in ages.

I turn on the news. The news is good on the one hand: *"we are not losing ground,"* and *"the Russians have heavy losses,"* but on the other hand: *"cruise missiles are flying at us from the territory of Belarus, and an armada of troops and tanks is rushing toward Kyiv through the Chernobyl zone from the territory of Belarus."* Belarus!!! How is that?

Breaking news: They show a Russian cruise missile hitting a multi-story building in Kyiv.

I must be asleep. This can't be happening. I watched the reports of wars in the former Yugoslavia, and in Georgia, but I have never seen anything like this. I can't go to bed. I'm not afraid. I'm just angry, very angry at myself, too, because I cannot help myself. I write to my colleagues from Russia, and I see that I am not the only one writing to them. Many of my Ukrainian colleagues write on their Facebook timelines and in comments. The Russians respond with silence. They pretend to see nothing. I am completely fucked up. Pavel Rudnev, the number one Russian

Screenshot. Photo 3.

A Dictionary of Emotions in a Time of War

theater critic, writes about Stanislavsky and the peculiarities of theater criticism, while ignoring our comments that we are being utterly wiped out here. Putin's rating has jumped 11 percent since the war began.

I take sedatives. I go outside. Maybe a pharmacy is open somewhere.

I go in the direction of my theater. The pharmacies are all closed. The city is quiet, only long, silent lines at grocery stores. I see my theater. I feel relieved. My home theater, and our flag flies above it. I'm so glad I came here.

On the way back, I meet Oleh Stefan with a backpack. He did not make it onto a train. In addition to the shelling, battles with invading groups of saboteurs have begun in the city. All the bridges are blocked, and the metro is operating exclusively as a bomb shelter. Kyiv's left and right banks are essentially two separate, isolated cities. We embrace. Who could have imagined meeting like this? We'll stick together now. We'll keep in touch.

We agree to celebrate his birthday the morning of the day after tomorrow at my place to spite all assholes.

We agree that, afterwards, we will go and take up automatic weapons, sign up for the territorial defense. Mom, forgive me.

I run home inspired. I need to calm down and get ready. For this I have a tried-and-true method: clean everything at home, mop the floors, open the windows, and ventilate the apartment, wash again the dishes that are already washed. These activities always clear my mind. All my thoughts fall into place.

Just one hour, more or less, out of the day. I run home, open the bedroom window for ventilation, turn on the news, clean up. My mobile phone rings. It's the owner of the apartment I rent: *"Pavlo, what are you doing there?"* A neighbor from our block has called him, complaining that I had opened the windows and was making loud banging noises. Another neighbor who is in the territorial defense wants me to approach my window carefully. I approach the window and show myself to a group of people with yellow armbands. I say I'm not making any noise. The owner says the neighbor wants to come in and see, to check things out. Of course, I agree. Let him come, I say. I've been living in this apartment for almost a year, and I recognize the neighbor's face. The owner knows who I am and what I do. At my invitation, he and his wife went with me to my theater to see one of my productions. They were all full of trust and love. The doorbell rings. I open up to see the muzzle of a submachine gun pointed at me, and three armed men in civilian clothes led by my neighbor who lied about my making noise. They point their weapons at me and run around my apartment, looking for saboteurs, whom they do not find. They remark that I should never have opened the window, because in this way I might send signals to someone (Putin I guess). I close the doors after these visitors leave. I close the windows, and, for the first time in this entire war, I feel fear, animal fear. I vomit. My day died at that moment. I spent the entire day, evening, and night just lying down. Indifferent to everything. No matter how many times air raid alarms sounded, a new reality drowned me out inside of myself. I know that these people I invited into my apartment did everything right. There is a war on in this city. Everyone is actively looking for the enemy. All those who took up arms are saintly people and real heroes, period. But I'm just a civilian. Who am I? I do nothing useful. I don't understand how to do anything. Thank you for the fact that on this day I realized I will not take a machine gun and I will not go enroll in the territorial defense. I will not be able to do that because we are not Switzerland. And we don't need to become Switzerland. We need to become ourselves. We are learning to be ourselves, and in order to become ourselves. We must learn on the basis of what is natural to us. Moreover, we must love, care, take responsibility, forgive, support, trust, respect, look into one another's eyes, be considerate, supportive, be honest, see the good (not just the bad), pity, understand, say kind things, be cheerful, help, admire, protect, etc. etc. But where will this line be, the one that separates what is natural to you or to others?

DAY FOUR
27 February 2022

At night, in addition to explosions, one can also hear ordinary shots. Beneath my windows at night, armed members of the territorial defense brigade dig trenches, haul in concrete blocks and sandbags, and set up roadblocks. My street's appearance has changed. It has become a street at war.

Fantastic morning news: We didn't just hold our defenses. We beat back the enemy, and very hard. The myth of the invincible Russian army is crumbling before our eyes. Putin's blitzkrieg has been canceled. Putin could not take a single city.

The whole world is up in arms, defending us. I feel hopeful. I feel inspired.

Photo 4.

My first call is to my mother: *"Mom, I'm alive! How are you doing? Did you hear the news?"*

My FB post: "Kyiv! Ukraine is holding on."

As for me, I realize I am a civilian, an ordinary resident of Kyiv, and this is also very important, for there are a lot of people like me. These people also need love, attention, and protection. I must discover my own way, my own resistance to the enemy who has attacked my Ukraine, my Kyiv, my life. This enemy attacked our conscience, our mutual respect, our kindness, our freedom, all the good things we had, have, and will have. This is what gives us meaning. This is the world we want for ourselves and that we wish for our loved ones.

Putin's world, or as he and his ideologues call it, the "Russian world," will fall apart precisely because it is based on such things as fear, pride, arrogance, envy, cunning, meanness, cruelty, and crazy lies.

That is what I believe. Faith keeps me afloat. I understand there is a certain bathos in my words, but after all . . .

A few days ago, I saw somewhere in my Facebook feeds a photo of Golda Meir, who was, incidentally, born in Kyiv, and was the prime minister of Israel during its struggle for the right to exist. Her words were printed beneath the photo: "Pessimism is a luxury that Jews cannot afford." It's the same with us now. And so everyone does what they can. We are different, but everyone is in their own place. Everyone is very necessary. This is our strength. Kyiv is a place of power!

I make my second call to my mother: *"Mom, I have to stay in Kyiv. I'm needed here. My apartment is here, my things, my work, my theater."*

FB post: "I am staying in Kyiv deliberately and there is no power capable of expelling me from here. Kyiv is mine!"

All my bridges are burned, and if I get scared and want to fucking run, I'll be too ashamed to do it. I'm in a great mood!

DAY FIVE
28 February 2022

The night passes, more or less . . . I manage to get four hours of sleep. Air raid alarms follow one after the other with only short intervals between them. Physically, I simply can't just run the hell down to the bomb shelter all the time anymore. I understand that this is wrong, you can't relax, and I'm doing it wrong. I'm home alone, so there's no one but me here to save. I just stay at home. I sit in the bathroom, stretching out in the tub, and sleep, if you can call it sleep. The main thing is to stay away from windows and window glass. Somewhere I heard that the bathroom is the best place.

I made this photo for my mother, so she would believe that I'm taking care of myself.

When I can't sleep, I binge-watch news. I try to watch not only ours but also German and American news. I try Russian too, but I can't stand it. They are just fucking Satanists living in a parallel reality.

Finally, my morning call to my mother: *"Mom, how are you? Why didn't you go down to the garage? Your basement isn't any good — it's an old apartment building made of concrete blocks. If anything, there'll be nothing but a couple of wet spots left of you. Mom, I love you very much. Go back to sleep."*

Today we celebrate Oleh Stefan's birthday at my apartment. Another neighbor and a colleague will come, too — the director Misha Uritskiy who lives next to Stefan. It's lucky they're here nearby and I'm not alone.

I prepare a festive pumpkin soup. The pumpkin has been here with me since pre-war times. I'll give Oleh "Colonialist

Photo 5.

Pearls," a bottle of expensive collectible sparkling wine that I have had since last year. I myself didn't know why I was hoarding it. Now I do. We'll drink it together. We'll try to live this day like normal people, as if everything here is just fine and dandy. I cleaned the apartment, warned the apartment owner that there would be guests, so he could warn my neighbor from the territorial defense, just in case. Oleh calls to say they have left. I will meet them halfway. It takes almost an hour for them to walk over here. I must meet them near our theater where we want to take a picture for our colleagues who are now far away. We also want to go to the store together, pick up some bread, cheese, maybe something else. It's a sunny day and it smells like spring. The photo shows Oleh and me against the backdrop of the theater where we work — the Kyiv Academic Drama and Comedy Theater on the left bank of the Dnipro River. Misha snaps the photos of us.

Photo 6.

A Dictionary of Emotions in a Time of War

FB post: "This is how we celebrate Stefan's birthday — with our theater, Kyiv, and Ukraine." Bathos again, sorry.

It is impossible to get into the store. The lines are very long.

We walk on until we reach my street, witnessing how the territorial defense catches either a looter or an invading terrorist. The young guy's arms are twisted harshly behind his back. A lot of people stand around at a safe distance, everyone watching in silence, a kind of outdoor theater performance. I wonder who the guy really is, what his story is. But we were afraid to ask, so now we can only imagine what happened. It probably is none of our business. He probably got into it himself and deserved what happened. But hell, I still don't feel good about it. We should have asked, but we just went on our way. Damn, I don't know what's right. My principles are getting blurry, too. It pisses me off.

I would prefer not fearing to talk to our military and territorial defense soldiers, if possible. If appropriate. If . . . If . . . If . . .

Oleh really wants to find bread for my pumpkin soup, but first of all, there are lines everywhere, second of all, there is no guarantee that there is bread in the stores.

I have some flour and drinking water at home, so Oleh decides to bake bread in a frying pan. Instead of a loaf of bread, it turns out to be like a Jewish matzo. That's the bread Jews ate when they came out of slavery. Very symbolic.

We eat soup and matzo in silence, and drink sparkling wine. We don't want to talk. We want to be together and keep quiet about something very important together. It is delicious, touching, and sinister.

Text messages began coming to my phone today from the State Emergency Service of Ukraine.

Photo 7.

Text Message 1: "Curfew begins today at 20:00. It is forbidden to be on the streets during the period of curfew. The only exception is moving to a shelter during an alarm. Follow the rules of blackout: Close windows, turn off lights."

A Dictionary of Emotions in a Time of War

DAY SIX
1 March 2022

Air raid alarms all night. Friends in chats, anybody else left in Kyiv write the warning: "Air."

Across from me is a park that looks more like a forest. Around two in the morning there is shooting. Saboteurs are spotted. I run to the bathroom, away from the windows.

Morning call to my mother: *"Everything is fine. Everyone is alive. I heard explosions but it hasn't reached my area so far, yet. I love you, Mom."* I don't tell my mother anything about the shooting. She's already just barely holding on.

A call from Israel, my nephew Marcus, who serves in the Israeli Defense Forces: *"It's not safe to hide in the bathroom, the tiles on the walls are just as dangerous as glass from windows."* Marcus helps me discover that the best place in my apartment is the entry corridor, bare walls, no windows. The mirror from the wall must be taken down and moved to another room for the duration of my stay. The more blankets and pillows the better. Be sure to sleep in clothes. Everything you need should be kept at hand.

I decide to go to the theater. It somehow calms me down, gives me meaning. I have very little food at home. Maybe I can buy something.

The checkpoint near the house has turned into a fortress of concrete blocks, metal structures, trucks, and sandbags. It's manned by a bunch of people with guns and yellow armbands. All cars are checked; pedestrians are not. It is strictly forbidden to take photos. So there are no photos of that here.

A pleasant surprise. The line disappeared at the big grocery store near me, so I went in. The store is selling air, completely empty shelves.

I go to a larger supermarket, usually a 20-minute walk. The bridge over the canal is blocked, so you need to take detours, and the walk now takes 45 minutes. There are people there, but not many. It quickly becomes clear why:

Photo 8, above: Bread shelves.

Shock — there are four million of us in Kyiv.

But there are sweets, and cookies, mostly very expensive and from abroad, but we do have some local things — marshmallows, for instance. And there are bananas. I buy ten bananas. I carry a full backpack. I won't starve to death, that's good. There is no bottled drinking water. I'll drink boiled tap water.

I don't want to think about bad things. I just want to go home. I'll sit there and think.

Photo 9, above right: Shelves for macaroni, grains, and dry goods.

The news from the fronts is good. Our army is doing well — a sea of destroyed enemy equipment, thousands of dead Orcs. Our authorities are constantly in touch with the populace. The president is doing a great job. The world is with

Photo 10, below right: Meat and fish.

us. Hellish sanctions against Russia. They promise food shipments will be made soon.

I'm only worried that I don't have blood pressure medicine. It's dangerous. A friend writes that a pharmacy is open in their area. I run over there.

3:45 p.m.: There is a pharmacy, and it's open. The line is long, but I have hope I'll get in before closing time. I stand there. The line is made up mostly of women. Everyone is nervous. Everyone needs something terribly. The line barely moves. People swear and curse at those who take too long. The necessary medicines are often not available, so pharmacists have to look for replacements. That's a problem. I understand everyone. I feel very sorry for everyone, but the atmosphere is terrible. An air raid alarm sounds, powerful explosions are heard quite close by

Photo 11.

and everyone is afraid. But no one leaves — medicines are too important. I stand in line for three hours. I understand this is pointless. Everyone in line is raging at one another. Everyone hates each other. Some people leave, realizing there is no chance of getting in.

I also want to leave, but I decide to wait it out until the end. And in a miracle of great humanity, it turns out that the head pharmacist promises to keep working until as late as possible, that is, until 7:30 p.m., because the curfew begins at 8 p.m. and the pharmacy employees must have time to run home.

The decision of the pharmacy employees affects the entire line. People become friendly to each other in an instant. They begin talking, writing lists of the medicines everyone needs, and passing them ahead to the pharmacists so they can prepare everything in advance. This accelerates the process significantly.

It's as though some human magic has happened. They did not have my pills, but they gave me some others — not what I needed, but I won't die. Ha-ha.

I race home at 7:55 p.m. I'm safe. I have food and medicine. My apartment is my fortress.

Russian ship, go fuck yourself! *"I'm in my own home."*

Conclusion of the day: humanity is not just a word. It works. The organization and interaction of people helps even where it seems there is no way out.

Thank you to the workers of the Be Healthy pharmacy. You are my heroes.

My words probably sound very pretentious again, even simplistic. I would not write like this in normal times. But I have a feeling that war, indeed, simplifies everything a lot, removes the masks from people behind which they hide in their normal lives. People become who they truly are, real and quite vulnerable, and all the good and bad falls out of us.

We receive a new text message from the state emergency service: "Your actions in case of an air raid alarm: Turn off electrical appliances, turn off gas and water.

— Turn off the lights, close the curtains.
— Move quickly to the nearest shelter. Take documents, money, and food.
Don't panic, warn your family and neighbors."

DAY SEVEN
2 March 2022

Morning: Call to my mom: *"Mom, How are you? Are you taking your sedatives? Mom, I see the news. It's impossible for a young man to leave now. I'll stay here. All my things are here. What if I can't get back? This is all I have. Plus I've already paid for the apartment a month in advance. I feel needed here. What will I find there? Mom, we already talked about this — you're starting it all over again. I can't stay at home all the time. I'm not a cat. Mom, please. Of course, call whenever you feel the need, every five minutes if you want."*

In order to stay in Kyiv, and at the same time not forget why I am here, not to go off the rails, not to do stupid things, not to let myself despair, I shall, from this moment forward, begin creating rules and rituals for myself. Should they be helpful, I will try to adhere to them, while those that do not work, I shall reject, and then seek new solutions.

Second rule: Never say never. If the situation worsens and there is a direct threat to my life, I must leave Kyiv and go to a safe place, if possible.

Third rule: Support family, friends, acquaintances, everyone with whom I communicate with words of support. Tell them about my warm feelings for them, emphasize their best qualities, support them in their decisions. I will definitely do this truthfully and sincerely through empathy, and not by uttering empty words and sentences.

First ritual: I will try to go to my theater every day. It truly calms me down and gives me a focal point in my everyday plan of affairs. I will tell my colleagues and friends about that. Maybe it will offer them support, too.

Second ritual: Get in touch with Oleh every morning and every evening. He is my friend, he is not far from me, and with him I feel I am not alone. I will do the same with Kostya Shakhman, a young actor from our theater. We are friends too. He is with his mother and incapacitated grandparents, also in Kyiv but on the right bank, so it is unrealistic to meet. It is very difficult for him both mentally and physically, but he finds the strength to talk, to support me, and I am very grateful to him for this. I also try to support and entertain him.

I was in the theater, or rather near the theater. I did not go inside, and I took a couple of photos. An air raid alarm sounded. There were loud explosions nearby, and I had to go to the underground floor of a nearby shopping center. As I waited and watched the news, my mood finally turned sour. I wanted to go home to my apartment, to my corridor as soon as possible, listen to the news in order to understand, but what I might understand I didn't know myself.

Late evening: I've lost count of how many air raid alarms there were today . . . An explosion near a train station with children and women was scary. This is my bunker, my entry hall here, probably the safest place for me in this reality. Good night, dear people. May we all see morning.

DAY EIGHT
3 March 2022

As was customary, the eighth day of the war for me began around three in the morning, with an air raid alert.

Most of the days and nights are accompanied by air raid alarms, and the sounds of explosions. Somehow I'm just now beginning

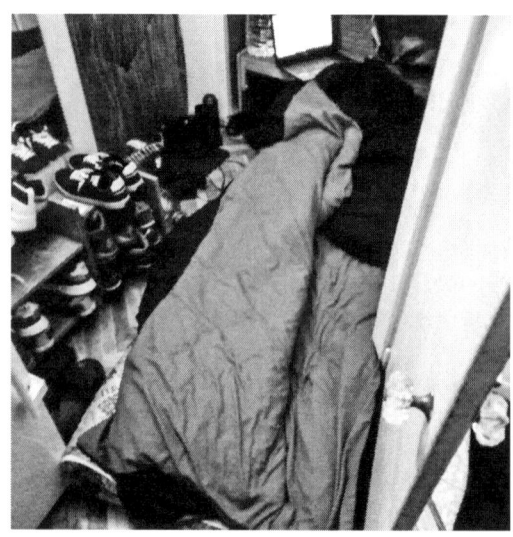

Photo 12.

to ignore them. It all becomes a kind of background noise around you and nothing more. I know this is a mistake, you can't do that, but the subconscious mind somehow grows tired of all this and just turns off on its own. Therefore, there's a new, fourth, rule: Don't fail to respond to air raid alarms. If you don't go to a bomb shelter, at least shelter in your own corridor, one without windows.

And, I want to come up with another, third, ritual . . . Many people advise you to pray when things get ominous or you get lonely.

I was taught well to say traditional prayers. I can do that, and I even want to. But, I can't. Praying in this situation seems to me to be infantile. You must rely only on yourself.

As you suffer from a lack of sleep, fatigue, and other sensations, you have the feeling that your point of view is expanding and you have the ability to see God himself out of the corner of your eye. I have that ability, but I don't see God. In my Facebook feed and in the news, I hear numerous cases about urban residents fleeing the war and not taking their dogs and cats with them. At best they just leave them on the street. Sometimes they lock them up in their apartments and leave. I don't understand how anyone can do this. I get dressed and go looking for abandoned animals, and find an object near my house that looks like a rocket.

Photo 13.

Text Message 4:
"The State Emergency Service of Ukraine informs you! If you find suspicious items or ammunition, do not attempt to disassemble them or move them to another location. Immediately inform the State Emergency Service, the Ministry of Internal Affairs, or the Armed Forces of Ukraine by calling 101, 102, 0800507028."

He said it turned out that the ammunition was new, not used. Someone had hidden it.

Photo 14.

The big city around me isn't just changing, it's deteriorating. That's what I think now. Since the first day of the war, all traffic lights have been turned off, garbage is rarely removed, and medicines and food are difficult to find.

Plus, weapons are now scattered everywhere, and poor theoretical pets are thrown out on the street.

The general mood is fair-to-middling. I want to hide from all this in my sleep. I'll get a good night's sleep if everything looks better.

DAY NINE
4 March 2022

I couldn't get enough sleep. I counted 13 air raid alarms during the day, and heard explosions very close by.

Mom calls: *"Son, I'm very worried . . ."*

"Don't overdo it, Mom. Everything is under control. I love you, Mom."

Oleh and Misha left Kyiv today, the last friends I could meet with. Of course, I'm glad they'll be safer. There are more and more explosions in Kyiv. Troops have been storming nearby villages and towns.

Because of fatigue, not apathy, I will try to tear myself away from the news and go to bed early.

DAY TEN
5 March 2022

During the night a powerful explosion goes off somewhere nearby. The house itself tossed me in the air. Sirens and alarms. The territorial defense bustles around the house in the midnight darkness. My head aches insanely — it will not let me get up from the floor. I pray. I pray not as I was taught to, but in the words that just pour out of me — a prayer like that, from the bottom of my heart:

Prayer during an air raid alarm

Ahh! How fucked up I am!
I wish upon them the most terrible death that exists!!!
I hate this!!!
Damn them to eternity and back, along with each and every one of their descendants!!!
Amen to that.
This concerns everyone who supports this, without the right to repentance or pardon!!!
Along with all their descendants.
May all their evil plans come back straight at them.
Amen.

And one more thing! I want to sleep! Let me sleep!

Text Message 5: The civilian population is prohibited from participating in military operations. It is prohibited to:

– go near windows if you hear gunshots;
– watch the fighting;
– stand or run under fire;
– enter conflict with armed people;
– wear military clothing;
– display weapons or any object similar to them;
– pick up abandoned weapons and ammunition.

DAY ELEVEN
6 March 2022

Irpin ((

Photo 15.

Photo 16. I recognize this place. I've been here twice on dates.

Text Message 6: If part of your building has collapsed:

— free your arms and legs;
— evaluate the situation;
— carefully remove any blockage without touching what is holding everything together;
— call for help;
— call or knock on pipes;
— give yourself first aid.

DAY TWELVE
7 March 2022

I am stressed out about all material things in my apartment, I just want to take it all to the trash — it's all superfluous and inappropriate. Of all the things I possess, the most valuable are old photos my mother once gave me...

Civilian services have begun picking up garbage again — that's a good sign.

I hear the sounds of war slowly moving towards my left bank from the direction of Brovarskiy Prospect.

Fighter jets fly loud and low, right overhead. They are ours, coming to attack... My body is frightened. My knees bend in my body, and my body is looking for a crack, any crack — anywhere to hide.

Photo 17.

Text Message 7: Actions in the event of an explosion near you:

— lie down on the ground and cover your head with your hands;
— avail yourself of available shelter;
— don't hurry to leave shelter;
— help the wounded;
— do not enter damaged buildings.

In the evening you will have to give your neighbor injections because the nurse has evacuated. There will also be an air raid alert, this time necessitating a descent to the basement. Later, the news will report that "two enemy fighters were shot down over Kyiv." Hooray!

And again there will be explosions, and sleep will come from 2 to 4 a.m. News about the bombing and rocket attacks on civilians in the densely populated cities of Ukraine do not let me sleep. They do not give me a single moment of peace. They do not let me breathe.

DAY THIRTEEN
8 March 2022

Abandoned

A play drawn from life

ACTORS:

I — *A 45-year-old man, 170.68 kilos, a civilian, with backpack. All in black.*

WOMAN — *Over 70. Intelligent looking. Breathes heavily, carries excess weight, walks leaning on a crutch with left hand. By all indications, she has diabetes.*

Rusanivska embankment, on the street near the last open grocery store in the area. Everyone in the long line freezes in the cold. There is almost no one on the street apart from those standing in line. It's getting late.

INTERNAL VOICE OF I: Even now I'm the same, you know, not at all mad at anyone. I want to be, but I can't. I'm torn by a completely different feeling. People are so fucking pathetic. Every one. I leave the house, or I come out of the basement after an air raid alarm . . . I walk in circles. I look at people, at ordinary people, those with no weapons, and I want to save them. I feel sorry for them, I utter some goddamned words of kindness, gentle-fucking-words . . . I carry their bags for them . . .

A woman overdid her purchases at the grocery store. She comes out with a crutch in her left hand, barely dragging two heavy bags of food.

I approach her. I stop. I hesitate. Start again . . . I go past the woman. Everyone goes their own way.

Now I'm catching up with the woman.

I. [*Breathing heavily*] May I help? Carry your bags?

The woman looks around. There's just the two of us. She holds her bags close to her body.

WOMAN. I'm okay.

INTERNAL VOICE OF I. She was so scared that I was totally confused. That's what made me speak such bullshit . . .

I. Don't be afraid, I'm a friend.

The woman hesitantly lets me take her bags.

WOMAN. It's not far.

I. I'm in no hurry. I'm alone here.

WOMAN. Did your family leave?

I. All I have is my mother, in Lviv.

WOMAN. Shouldn't you go to her?

I. I'm feeling better here now.

WOMAN. But your mother would probably prefer you be together.

I. Yes, but it's very hard to leave. It's all only for women with children.

WOMAN. Yes. My daughter and granddaughter wanted to leave yesterday. We tried getting in a taxi, here at the Darnitskiy railway station.

I. And why couldn't you?

WOMAN. [*Excited*] There was a huge crowd. My daughter and granddaughter were able to get in. But me with my weight, my legs are sore. Instead of helping me, people pushed me away. I fell to my knees and got up only later.

I. That's terrible.

WOMAN. My daughter and granddaughter left. I stayed. But I'm very happy that she's safe. That's important . . .

I. I'm sorry, but that's wrong.

WOMAN. No, no, I don't feel abandoned.

I. But people . . . I'm so sorry.

WOMAN. I've already lived my life. People are frightened. And I'm almost not afraid at all. You see, I bought groceries. They'll last a few weeks. It's very hard for me to walk.

We walk in silence.

INTERNAL VOICE OF I. I'm looking for words to keep the conversation going, but I have nothing to say to her. I'm ashamed as if I was the one who had pushed her down at that train station.

WOMAN. Here we are.

I. I'll see you to your floor.

The woman and I stand by the landing before the door.

I. First I'll set your packages down here, then you can open your door. After all, I'm a stranger.

WOMAN. Yes, and what's your name?

I. Pavlo.

WOMAN. Pavel? Well, my name is Vera Pavlovna. My father was Pavel.

INTERNAL VOICE OF I. Tears flow from Vera Pavlovna's eyes. Vera Pavlovna is crying.

I. Don't cry, Please.

VERA PAVLOVNA. I thought I was alone, I was abandoned. But now, here you are, Pavel. My father sent you to me.

INTERNAL VOICE OF I. I do not know what to say to her. Tears are streaming from my eyes. Vera Pavlovna and I stand and cry. I so want to tell her: "Yes, daughter, I am your father."

DAY FOURTEEN

Bucha. Irpen . . .
I am empty, I have nothing to say.
Listening to Olena: https://youtu.be/PEtg5j9xUyA.

DAY FIFTEEN
TIME HAS STOPPED

Location: Kyiv Academic Drama and Comedy Theater on the left bank of the Dnipro River.

"Frozen Time" is a mostly metaphorical concept that we use to try to describe our personal, inner state after experiencing some kind of shock. But this expression also has a metaphysical meaning, although people don't experience it often, for, as a rule, the phenomenon is associated with events that are more global and catastrophic, the kind that suddenly stop the movement of life so that nothing else happens, not even destruction, for destruction is also life in movement. As a rule, after a cataclysm, everything dies and is destroyed, and something new begins. That is, time goes on by itself, for those who remain live on for themselves. It is not enough when a person leaves everything as it was, in its place, and disappears. We can physically feel stopped time by seeing Pompeii dug out of the ground, Angkor Wat discovered in the jungles, or visiting the hastily abandoned city of Chernobyl, where radiation forced people to drop everything and leave. All these places make us feel something incomprehensible because the supernatural, the bizarre, the hostile is happening here. Because what can make you drop everything and leave? At the entrance to the theater where I work, through the window, under the inscription "Today," you see a poster of the performance that is to be performed in the evening. On February 24, a performance based on the last thing I had written, *Odysseus Comes Home*, was supposed to have been performed. All tickets were sold out, and the poster hanging there now had been posted the night before. But war broke out in Ukraine at four in the morning, and Kyiv was made the target of bombs and rocket attacks. Time flies in somersaults. My country is not conquered, but it is destroyed, destroyed by the aggressor. Some escape, some take up arms. Kyiv is fighting madly for survival. It is the fifteenth day of the war. I am the last of the employees who can come to work because I live nearby. I do it to calm my nerves, so as not to lose hope. The theater stands in place, and, behind a glass window, for the fifteenth day in a row, a poster announces a performance for today that simply cannot seem to come about.

JFr & NB

IN THE BOWELS OF THE EARTH
OLENA HAPIEIEVA

*Voices:

OLENA (Lena) and her two boys, **SVIATOMYR** (5 years old)
and **MYROSLAV** (not yet two)
DIMA – 35 years old
LIUBA, Dima's wife, and her son **BOHDAN**, 4 years old
AUNT SVETA – Liuba's mother
A CHUBBY FAMILY – MOM, DAD, their two young sons,
ANTON and **STIOPA**, both 5 years old
COURAGEOUS YOUNG WOMAN
NERVOUS WOMAN 1 AND HER HUSBAND
NERVOUS WOMAN 2 AND HER HUSBAND
SCHOOL PRINCIPAL
PEOPLE IN THE BOMB SHELTER – voices

---

* This translation retains the author's unorthodox format, including centered text, that mixes identified speech, unidentified speech, descriptions and "stage directions" into a single, flowing narrative.

A siren. My children and I go down into the bomb shelter.
The man from territorial defense points the way:
"To the left with small children, without children —
to the right."
OLENA. Why?
"There is a deeper basement for children."
OLENA. Okay, thank you.

Women with children go into a deeper basement. Adults go into a specially equipped bomb shelter with benches.

My children and I descend a ragged metal ladder.
There are women here with bags on wheels. Strange, I think,
hiding under the ground. The earth takes us in.
I recall the words of a woman, a veteran, a spy in World War II:
*"The earth protects us when things are bad or frightening, Lena.
Cling to the earth."* We descend into the earth's bowels.
I hide my children in it. We are looking for a place
to sit, we look around.

NERVOUS WOMAN 1. Shut up. Listen, we're in a bomb shelter.
Quit weeping and wailing. Sit quietly. Don't whine. Look at all the people here.
I don't know now what to do with you. Shush, now! Go to sleep, I said!

OLENA. Are these free?
"What?"

OLENA. The chairs, are they taken?
"No, take what you want.
Why are you howling again! Where are you going?
It's dirty there! Hey, I told you, sit in your stroller.
Your clothes are clean. I just put them on you today. Dad, where are you going? Say something to her."
"What can I say? And what can I do?"
"You don't even want to calm down your child. I'll spank you now! Sleep, I said. Sit still."
"She's going to fall out!"
"Rock her yourself! Go ahead! You think this is easy? Where are you going! Lie down, I said!!!"

When troops were stationed on the borders, I did not believe a full-scale war would begin. That is, I hoped it would not begin. In my opinion, February 22, 2022, and February 23, 2022, were the dangerous days. The former because it was a mirrored astronomical date, and the latter because it was Soviet Soldier Day. When I went to bed on the evening of the 23rd, I breathed a sigh of relief — "The war didn't start, ooof, Putin bluffing the West again." About 2 o'clock in the morning I woke up because a sewing needle was stuck in my side. I got up, sleepy, pulled it out of the sofa. Sure enough, a needle, it's sticking out of an armrest cover. "What is that doing in a child's bed?" At about 7 a.m., I leaped up in fright: the wall between our apartment and the neighbor's was shaking. Explosions could be heard in the distance. "Training exercises? Why didn't we hear this before, then? Why today? What happened?" I asked my neighbor. "Lena, war has begun."

NERVOUS WOMAN 2. Is this your child? [*She asks in Russian.*] He touched my baby bottle . . .
OLENA. Why you are shouting at him? I don't understand. Tell me . . .
"He touched it with his dirty hands. This is for a baby . . ."
"Quit yelling at him . . . How could he do that? How could you do that?"
"He touched it with his dirty hands. It's a bottle for a baby. Why are you grabbing other people's things?"
"I repeat: Speak to me. Don't yell at my child."

"Do you hear what I'm saying?" I ask. [*She continues to speak in Russian.*]
"Don't touch!"
"Say that to me!"
"Go fuck yourself!"
"You go fuck yourself!"

Her husband smiles a guilty smile and holds a little girl in pink.
The girl is two or three months old.
Ukrainian soldiers recently told a Russian warship "to go fuck itself."
Everyone is nervous. Children are crying. An air raid alarm sounds.
People stream into the basement of the school.

SVIATOMYR. Mom, I just wanted to look.
OLENA. Don't touch other people's things! Right, Liuba?
LIUBA. Come here to us, we're a little higher.
OLENA. Is it okay that we won't be in a deeper basement? What if it really does cave in?

SVIATOMYR. Mom, Mom, I want to go see Bohdan. He has a bunch of cool cars.
OLENA. Phew ... It's stuffy in here. These transmitters and pipes ...
LIUBA. It's the school's boiler room. Mother and I set up here especially for the children. It won't get cold at night.
SVIATOMYR. Mom, it's like a space station!
OLENA. Okay then, I'll bring my things. Will you have room to sit?
LIUBA. Bohdan can sleep here, Sviatik and Myron over here.
OLENA. Your mom, isn't she on chemotherapy now?
AUNT SVETA. Oh, no, Lenochka. It's all right. Everything is fine.
OLENA. The sirens went off today in the middle of the night. How do you sleep?
AUNT SVETA. We get a little sleep. It's nothing.
LIUBA. Where is Dima with the suitcases?
OLENA. What are they saying? An air raid or tanks?

"It seems they're coming from Kherson. They want to surround us."

OLENA. Where do you read that? Can I subscribe? In Telegram?

"Here, Vitaliy Kim. He's chairman of the Mykolaiv regional administration. He describes everything happening in Mykolaiv."

LIUBA. Tanks are headed for Mykolaiv ... Bohdan, here, have some cheese. Dima, what are you doing with that bag? What do you see in there?

[*An entire shelf is occupied by the Chubby Family: Husband, wife, and two sons — Stiopa and Anton. They speak in Russian.*]

FATHER. Why do you keep poking your mother? Can't you see she's busy? She's reading. I'm busy too. Either sit here or lie down — like Stiopa. Why are you so jumpy all the time? I told you, sit down.
ANTON. It hurts, Daddy.
FATHER. I said, don't whine. Now, hush. Sit! Sit down. Would you sit down!!
ANTON. It hurts, Daddy!!!
FATHER. Shush! Shush, I told you!!!
[*The boy cries.*]
Once and for all, would you sit down?!

OLENA. I don't like men like that!
AUNT SVETA. They want their children to sit at attention, while they hang out on their telephones.
LIUBA. He made himself at home. They took over all the children's places, and now when children come, there's nowhere for them to lie.
AUNT SVETA. The grown-ups all squeeze in, and you can be damned! What do you do with people like that?!

FATHER AND MOTHER. [*Simultaneously*] Your youngest child is about to fall. He constantly cries. Here, have a banana . . .

SVIATOMYR. Mom, take it. I want a banana . . . Oh, you have sandwiches, too. Can I have a sandwich? I'm hungry.

MOTHER. Here, have a banana.
OLENA. No thank you. He doesn't want it anymore.
FATHER. Take one for your youngest. Maybe he won't cry so much.
OLENA. He can't sleep. He wanders around bumping into walls, like a zombie. The air raid alarms scare him. Thank you . . .

LIUBA. Would he like a sandwich?
OLENA. I wanted to go to the store — but I never made it. I heard a siren, grabbed Myroslav in his sleep, a sleeping bag, and I ran.
AUNT SVETA. Here's some sausage, bread, cheese, and yogurt for the children, some cream cheese.
DIMA. I have a pot of boiling water.
LIUBA. Dima, where have you been? Can't you help me with the baby? What did you bring? We have hot water. I thought at least here he would help me, but no, he's out running around and smoking with the guys . . .

AUNT SVETA. Here, Sviatik, have a sandwich. Don't you want one? What else will you eat? Aren't you breastfeeding now?
OLENA. We brought nothing with us . . . I wasn't prepared . . . I never made it to the store . . . All the grocery stores and shops were closed.
SVIATOMYR. I'm hungry. Can I have a sandwich?
OLENA. Listen, shhh, we didn't bring anything.
LIUBA. No, no, enough of that. Have some, Sviatik.
SVIATOMYR. Oh, cool, that's good!
AUNT SVETA. Lena, have something else, maybe — you're breastfeeding.

OLENA. I don't eat bread. It's all right. Thank you so much. All right, I'll have some bread with this cheese. Myroslav doesn't want anything . . .

OLENA. More people coming in now. Tanks are firing — oh, there was a good pop.
SVIATOMYR. Mom, Mom — sirens, I'm afraid.
AUNT SVETA. More people coming in . . . There are no more chairs left. There are a lot of people today.

SVIATOMYR. What does the siren-sound do? Ooo-ooo . . . Mom, does it want to kill us?
OLENA. No, son, the siren warns us about danger — ooo-ooo — then people run for basements and bomb shelters. See? Here they come running.
SVIATOMYR. So the siren-sound helps us. Then who wants to kill us?
OLENA. Putin and the Russians are bombing our cities. They want to kill us.
SVIATOMYR. I understand. They must be dinosaurs. Mom, I am afraid.
OLENA. Dinosaurs died out a long time ago.
SVIATOMYR. Then who wants to kill us?
OLENA. Evil people, son.
SVIATOMYR. Who are these Russians?
OLENA. They are people from a neighboring country that hate us.
SVIATOMYR. Why?
OLENA. Because we are free, son.
SVIATOMYR. What's that?
OLENA. Well, we have our own opinion, our own land, and we love and defend it.

SVIATOMYR. What if a bomb falls on us?
OLENA. Don't be afraid. We are underground, and we are safe.
SVIATOMYR. In a hole in the ground?
OLENA. Yes.
SVIATOMYR. And it protects us?
OLENA. It covers us like this [*spreads hands over child's head*].
SVIATOMYR. Mommy, I don't want to die.
OLENA. No, no, you will live a long and happy life.
SVIATOMYR. And no Russians will kill me?
OLENA. No, son, they won't kill you. Our soldiers are fighting them.
SVIATOMYR. Those ones with wings?
OLENA. Remember when Daddy's friends came to visit —
Myron, Kid, and Oleh?
SVIATOMYR. They brought me a Kinder Surprise and a mechanical toy bear.
OLENA. Vitaliy, Ihor, and the doctor from Poltava.
SVIATOMYR. And Daddy?
OLENA. And Daddy . . .
SVIATOMYR. My daddy is fighting those dragons?
OLENA. That's right, son. Your daddy is fighting them.
He won't let those soldiers kill us and take away everything we have.
SVIATOMYR. My toys, my books, my computer.
OLENA. Our home, our way of life, our language, and who we are.
SVIATOMYR. But who are we, Mommy?
OLENA. Ukrainians.
SVIATOMYR. Ah, we're Ukraine!
We are Ukraine! We are Ukraine! [*Runs around and shouts to all.*]
OLENA. Everyone is going to hate me here.

MOTHER. Anton, come now, sit. Tell your father now, what do you want? Come here. He's allowed to. You're not.
Sit here. Next to Stiopa.

OLENA. The boy is bothering everyone. He's throwing a tantrum.
LIUBA. That angry old guy is shouting, "Whose child is that?!"

"We are Ukraine! We are Ukraine!"

Shelling in all cities. Ukraine has gone underground. Maybe the earth will protect us. I heard from a priest that prayers underground have especial power, so monks dug underground caves to pray in. I don't know how to pray properly, so I just make up prayers in my own words to block out the fear.

LIUBA. Bohdan, Bohdan, at least eat something, sweetheart. Here's an apple, a cookie. You haven't eaten all day. Mom, what am I supposed to do with him?!
OLENA. The little tyke just clings to me. So much stress, so many people, my teeth chatter. My chest hurts.
AUNT SVETA. The two of them are sprinkling sand on someone.
LIUBA. I'll go get them.
MOTHER. Talk to him. I can't calm him down.
FATHER. Come here, I said. How long will you keep this up?
ANTON. Daddy, don't . . . [*Father whacks him on the shoulder and shakes him. The boy cries.*] I want to go with him!
Sit down, I said. And sit there.
FATHER. Look, Stiopa is sitting and playing. [*Mother immediately hugs Stiopa and strokes him on the head.*]

MOTHER. Stiopa, Stiopushka, everything is all right . . .
ANTON. Mom . . .
MOTHER. Sit down, Anton.

AUNT SVETA. I waited so long for chemotherapy . . . it was possible to pay immediately, but a single sitting costs 40 thousand grivens, and you have to go through many . . . if you want to receive free treatment, you have to wait — and I waited forever. I just went in to do an IV — and the war started.
I only have one T-shirt with me.
OLENA. Good God, this child is a devil. Stop it! Put that back.
What are you putting in your mouth?!
Knives, nails, they're all dirty. [*He throws a piece of metal in the corner. People are startled. Silence, ringing silence, broken by a distant explosion.*]

Ka-boom!!!

CHORUS OF VOICES.
"Be silent if you can. Everyone's nerves are frayed!"
"A man is ill."
"Call an ambulance."

AUNT SVETA. Whoever thought this would come about!

"I didn't believe war would come until the very end."
"I think it will end tomorrow."
"Oh, they say it's going to be a long time."
"But there can't be a real war in our times, like there was with the Germans."

"This war is already underway."
"What does he care about anybody? He's sick in the head."
"I always thought Russia had a good president."
"They're bombing Kharkiv, bombing Kyiv, Chernihiv, Sumy, Mariupol...
battles are raging in Kherson, tanks are approaching Kyiv —
all at the same time."
"And they lie and lie and lie."
"They said they're going to catch Nazis, but they keep dropping bombs on the
heads of peaceful people."
"What did we do wrong? Why such a disaster on our heads? What did we do?"
"I had a premonition about this war. I told my sister:
Don't remodel your apartment, but she insisted. So what happens now?"
"They had just put in such beautiful new roads. Now they're tearing them
all to shreds."
"We should have invested in our army. Our neighbor has gone mad."
"Knock it off with the politics!"

[*The man can't take it anymore. He spits in disgust and moves to another corner of the shelter.*]

AUNT SVETA. Listen — air raid alarm again . . .
OLENA. Don't be afraid, son. We're with people here. Look at all the people hiding here from the war.
SVIATOMYR. Mom, I'm scared.

LIUBA. Here comes the school principal. What could she want?

SCHOOL PRINCIPAL. I ask all of you to turn off geolocaters on your phones, if they are turned on, and in Viber . . . yes, that's right, the VPN, right here.
Okay, you have a peer-to-peer connection. Fine.
We don't want them tracking where crowds are gathered.

AUNT SVETA. What a mother-in-law I had! Her husband's brother came to her once and started getting up on his high horse — she didn't bat an eyelash and gave him a good whack between the eyes. Showered him with blows, with whatever she could get her hands on. He fell, and cracked his head, and started bleeding, and everybody says. What have you done? You killed him! He lay there for a good, long time. He couldn't get up, and everyone thought he was dead. *"What of it?"* my mother-in-law says. *"They can put me in jail, but I'm going to stand up for myself."* Great mother-in-law, I learned a lot from her. Now, Liuba's mother-in-law is nothing like that. Cunning, lying, never helps with anything, and always makes out as if everything's Liuba's fault.

[*Voices fill the space of the bomb shelter:*]

"Putin is a cornered rat now. He's going to bite hard."
"I'm terribly afraid of a nuclear strike."
"All his rockets have long been aimed at Europe and America. That's why they won't come help us."
"They're afraid themselves."
"How my husband loved me. I can't tell you all the gifts he showered on me. Then somehow, I found out he had another woman. Naturally, I met with her — she was very young and beautiful. Smoky black hair, and dark eyes.

I talked to her. It was a calm, but firm conversation. After that she disappeared. Obviously, I got no more gifts, and the passion was gone. We began to live simply and calmly."
"They say there are going to be air strikes. We need to sit tight."
"Maybe there won't be?"
"What will they stop at? He's already broken everything! Children are dead, churches destroyed."
"They can fuck off, for all I care."
"That's for sure, only we're going to have to run them out. They won't go on their own."

"We ought to move closer to that wall over there. This one is on the street side, and it will collapse quickly. That other one should hold out."

[*People move to the stronger wall.*]

COURAGEOUS YOUNG WOMAN. "How about letting the women and children go first? Hey!"

MOTHER AND FATHER. Take your child. He'll fall off the stairs.
OLENA. And where do I put him?
AUNT SVETA. He won't sit still.
MOTHER AND FATHER. Ours sit still. See there? He fell, and he's crying. Quit jumping around! Sit still! Listen here! Sit still, Anton!
ANTON. It hurts, Daddy. Mommy! Mommy!

AUNT SVETA. [*Quietly, restrained*] They say Putin is like that because no one cared about him. His mother was a prostitute and left him to someone else's aunt, and she didn't care about him either. And that's how he grew up. Dull, damaged, clumsy, miserable. He was a no-count who gave everyone a hard time. His nickname was "moth."

He came to power in ragged pants.

Nobody wants a kid like that, you know, and that's how they grow up. You don't have to kiss their ass, but you do have to love them.

[*Voices:*]
"They say this is only the beginning."
"We'll sit here until tomorrow morning, if not longer."
"Those sounds . . ."
"What do you expect? It's war!"
"Oh, God. Oh, God!"
"In Sumy they came right into a bomb shelter and wanted to take everyone hostage."
"Are you kidding?"
"But the territorial defense pushed them back."
"Do you think they'll come in here, now?"

[*"Mommy, Mommy, I'm afraid," shout several children's voices.*]

COURAGEOUS YOUNG WOMAN. "Stop it!!! Don't scare the children. So what if they come! We're not just going to sit here twiddling our thumbs!"

These last words were spoken by a beautiful young woman, tall and straight as a tree, with her one-year-old baby, Davyd, in her arms. Silence reigns.

"You hear that? Planes coming. Something exploded in the distance. Gone . . ."

[*A whistle.*]

"Coming back."

AUNT SVETA. You know what, Lena? I would kill the occupiers. Bohdan, grandson, have an apple . . .
LIUBA. He doesn't want it. What can you do? You can't, you can't force a boy. Bohdan, don't be afraid.
AUNT SVETA. You think Liuba would kill? Yes, Liuba?
LIUBA. Dima, could you look after Bohdan for a while, give me a rest. Where do you go all the time? What time is it, Dima? Are you already drinking coffee? Yes, Mom, I would kill.

I remember the crumbly black earth in my grandmother's garden.
It had such an intoxicating smell. Your hands would be dry, black, and cracked.
Now we all sit in the bowels of the earth. The earth protects.
It hides. It covers. Ukrainians are defending this earth with their weapons.
The occupiers' boots tread on this earth. Such young men from the Russian hinterlands. Stupid and aggressively naive.
They want to take someone else's land. They stomp on the graves of my forebears. They burn them with fire and level them with the earth.
They themselves fall and smolder on the earth.

The earth burns their feet, breaks their hearts.
It dissolves in space and time. The earth clearly recognizes its own.
I lie face down on the earth in my grandmother's garden. I absorb it through my nostrils, like all the love I have ever known.

JFr & NB

Commissioned by a grant from Philip Arnoult's Center
for International Theatre Development

PLANTING AN APPLE TREE
IRYNA HARETS

Dwarf breeds of apple trees. They take up less space, and they match my height. They bloom and smell wonderful in the spring, when I can approach them and smell their blossoms without climbing up on a ladder. In the fall I will collect their sweet fruits. Sources on the Internet say the trees will bear fruit in the third year after the seedlings are planted. I'll wait. The main thing is to talk with my neighbor. He has a tractor, and we have abandoned, overgrown land. We recently bought a house with land in a village. We threw all our efforts into remodeling the house but never touched the land. We spent a long time thinking about what would grow here.

The distance between trees should be three meters, and the depth of the planting hole seventy centimeters.

"Can you imagine?" says my husband. *"They are just children playing war."* We stand calmly on this starry night, and suddenly hear sirens — an air-raid alarm. *"Drones, drones,"* men shouted and began running to their cars all over the village. I say, *"People, those are stars, twinkling stars."* The boys correct me, *"Drones, drones, they're moving."* I found an article on Wikipedia for them about the twinkling of stars, and I dropped it in the general chat of the territorial defense. We'll see what they write now. My husband laughs and hands me a phone with a chat open in Viber, where the men from territorial defense check their duty time, their team, and share the news.

In fact, I'm ashamed to go to our neighbor and ask point blank, *"Will you plow our land? Of course I'll pay you. Those who sold us the house, the former owners, said you always helped. Please help us."* I didn't dare even when my three-year-old granddaughter and I saw him as we passed by his hut and tractor. I just said hello. People greet each other in this village with such affection. Children say, *"Happiness and health"* instead of hello, or good afternoon. Adults add, *"God grant you health."* I still say, *"Good afternoon,"* or *"good evening."* But I will learn. My Varia and I were out for a walk, and we came upon a neighbor, said hello, and encountered a worm. A long, fat one crawling across the road. My granddaughter decided it was in danger because cars were driving past, and we watched for almost an hour as the worm slowly squirmed along, and we asked cars to go around it. Finally the worm got to the other side of the road and climbed under a leaf. Varia happily continued our walk. She is very smart for her age. She is capable of saying marvelous things.

"Where is your mommy?" she asks me.

"She died," I answer.

"Then, who is going to hug you and pity you?"

Then she said she remembered what it was like to be dead. Varia says she was dead, she couldn't move her legs and arms. And she saw nothing.

I don't cry. No tears flow. I just feel a fierce anger. My imagination paints a picture of a cluster bomb flying into the high-rise building where my children live, and killing my son-in-law, daughter, my Varia, and my little Orchik, who is less than a year old.

Discard the top layer of soil separately, then mix the soil with peat and humus, then add to the mixture some superphosphate and wood ash. Hammer a peg into the middle of the hole, then add the soil mixture. Over that sprinkle earth from the topsoil. Place a seedling in the center of the hole and separate its roots. It is very important that the roots do not touch the fertilizer, for it can burn the tree's delicate roots.

And, my husband says, rumors reached his soldiers that a party of Russians had landed. There was general excitement as plans were made to neutralize them. Then came the realization that they did not even have guns. They began thinking about what to do. I offered to stick a pitchfork upside-down in the ground, pointing upwards. Let the assholes plant themselves on that.

I will come to you on a tank, says my uncle from Moscow. You are fascists and Nazis. You must be destroyed. Oh, yes, Uncle Sasha, women with babies in the maternity ward in Mariupol are your greatest enemy. You have destroyed the heart of fascism and Nazism in our country. And the grandmothers who sit in the basements of Okhtyrka, and the small children you killed, and people with disabilities who do not have access to medicine.

I don't cry. They say it's easier when tears flow, even more useful.

We have a quiet region. Sirens ring out periodically, but we haven't been bombed yet. I even feel guilty that my sister is being bombed in Kharkiv, and my family is being bombed in Kyiv. I try not to think about the many places where people are on the verge of a humanitarian catastrophe, without water, food, medicine, and where children die of dehydration. I take in refugees almost every day. Tired people with frightened eyes. A five-year-old boy asked to watch cartoons. He sat quietly, watching. Suddenly the cartoon's music imitated the sound of a siren, and the child dashed and scrambled under the bed. *"Mommy,"* he cried plaintively. Later there were many other such children and adults. I do not have time to air out the bed. I never finish the process of cooking. I am running out of internal resources.

Fatigue. I don't cry. No tears flow.

After planting it in the ground, you tamp down the soil around the seedling, and at a distance of half a meter from the trunk, you build a ridge around it 15 centimeters high. In the resulting depression you pour in 25 to 30 liters of water.

I'm ashamed to admit it, but on the first day of the war I had diarrhea and was sick to my stomach. I thought I had been poisoned by something. I thought if a bomb flew into the house, I would die awkwardly, pants down on the toilet. A silly death. The days go by like years. It seems like a peaceful life is something distant and unattainable. But I have an abundance of patience and anger. I also have an abundant supply of pills that I cannot live without. If they run out, I will die a nasty death over a period of three months. The Internet says I eventually will just fall asleep. At least I'll finally get some sleep. I don't want to cause problems that might make my relatives worry. I do not want to be a weak link, a burden, if our city is surrounded. I do not know how people live with my diagnosis, and without pills when surrounded by an enemy. Be patient, my dears. Be patient, we will win. I try not to think about those who need insulin. Their situation is much worse than mine. They don't have three months left.

Since the root system in this kind of apple tree clings to the surface ... Today, again, diarrhea and nausea. I just went to vomit. But what about the apple trees? Aha, we must not let the roots dry out. Constant watering and mulching. I need to note everything down in writing. That will be my witness when I forget.

My nephew in Moscow, five-year-old Andriusha, stayed with his nanny, found a portrait of Putin, took scissors, cut it into small pieces, and said, *"Die, scum!"* The nanny was frightened, scolded his parents, and warned him not to do that in kindergarten.

One needs love and humanity in these days of rage and hatred. My youngest daughter is pregnant and terribly frightened. She called to tell me there was an air raid alarm, and because she was on the street and did not know where to hide, my arms and legs began to tremble. But it's no big deal, no big deal, I repeat to myself constantly. It's nothing, you just must wait, struggle, and suffer the pain. It's like giving birth. Then you look at the baby and think, *"Wow, good for me! I did it!"* We will cope. I want to balance anger with love and tenderness. My pregnant Dasha picked up a little mutt named Bun at the shelter. Bun entertains my child and relieves some of the anxiety. My husband

and I also picked up a dog, Squirrel. We love our little one, although, to be honest, she looks like a little bat. Most important, the formerly homeless Bun and Squirrel are full of love for us. You need balance.

My grandmother, who is half Tatar, was supposed to inherit a huge apple orchard from her Tatar grandparents. But she didn't. First, the Soviet government took away the apple orchard, and destroyed the trees. Second, even if she had managed to inherit it, she would not have been allowed to do anything, acquire a profession or earn a living.

I think, could it be my fault that the war started? Maybe my thoughts about the new apple orchard reflected some absolutely evil universe, a kind of Mordor that rejects everyone who loves, creates, and generates something. That destroys for centuries anything that is capable of creating happiness and giving life.

When watering the apple tree, take care with the supports under the fruit-laden branches.

JFr & NB

Commissioned by a grant from Philip Arnoult's Center for International Theatre Development

FLOWERING
OLHA MACIUPA

Voice Of A Plant That Doesn't Want To Be Uprooted From The Earth:

I've been to Paris, but never to Donetsk. I've been to Munich, but never to Kherson. I've been to Rome, but never saw the old monuments of Chernihiv. There are many cities on the map of Ukraine I've never been to. Some are already completely destroyed. I always wanted to go on a big trip around Ukraine, but kept saying let's go to Croatia, let's go to Europe; Ukraine won't go anywhere. I'd work, do some maintenance on the flat, buy a car, more maintenance, then — let's go to Europe; Ukraine won't go anywhere. Then came a pandemic, then war. Will there be a famine? Ukrainians remember times of breadlessness in previous generations — especially the artificial famine of 1932–1933. The man I love always carries a small cracker in his pocket. He always has a little piece of bread, wherever he goes.

I visited Sievierdonetsk two weeks before the start of the full-scale war. Yes, I was in Donbas then for the first time in the eight years of war. Sievierodonetsk is the easternmost Ukrainian city I've ever been to. The name comes from the name of the river Siverskyi Donets — the Donets, one of my favorite rivers. This deep river in the east is where I saw real water lilies for the first time. So white, so gentle, with a yellow middle. It is as if the sun floats on the water and looks at its reflection in the sky. I read on the Internet that the rhizome of the plant can protect people who go to foreign lands. It must be dried then held near the heart as an amulet.

The Choir Of Death Of Russian Imperial Structures:

Hey, you steppe flowers
Which bloomed so well
in the dark chernozem soil!
Hey, you steppe flowers
And you, deep water
Flowing into the sea —
We have come to protect you!
We have here our orders
To trample you with tanks,
To stir up the post-industrial wind,
To spit at you with Kalashnikovs,

To hurl missile damage at you.
We will call it our own.
We will invent toxic family ties,
Toxic brotherhood,
And if you refuse
Then in the name that we give you,
We will kill you.
But there is a risk
We will all perish from the post-industrial
Wind and fire.

Voice Of A Plant That Doesn't Want To Be Uprooted From The Earth:

It was at Saltiv in the Kharkiv region that I tried paddleboarding for the first time. With the man I love. We sailed in a wooden boat there too. The water lilies were so close — so white, so beautiful. That was in 2012, when the European Football Championship match between Ukraine and Poland took place, the end of the world had not come, and it seemed everything would be fine. It was such a beautiful summer and for a short time it seemed that we were about to be in the European Union. At least we chose this direction. For such a short time, it seemed everything would be fine. We would not have to line up in humiliating queues for visas at consulates and at borders. We would be able to study freely in Europe, go on residencies, create art. Let's go to Europe — Ukraine won't go anywhere, we will always have time. These hopes came to an end in the fall of 2013, when students were beaten up in the main square of Kyiv. The nightmare began. And continues. Now there are Russian tanks in Saltiv. The city of Vovchansk — where the person I love comes from — is occupied. It's in the Kharkiv region.

The Donets flows from Saltiv to Donbas, and yes, I was in Donbas, in Sievierodonetsk, two weeks before the full-scale Russian invasion. It was February 12, my father's birthday, and I was close to the line for the first time in my life. I didn't give any gift to my dad; I just congratulated him — our family doesn't pay much attention to gifts.

I had long wanted to go east. I had such an inner need, and besides I had a theatrical premiere there. I had an inner need to go to my favorite eastern river. Many friends from Poland said I was crazy because there were Russian tanks on the border. And it's not safe. But the last eight years were also dangerous. In Sievierodonetsk, people have already seen the war with their own eyes, heard it with their own ears, and know how to behave during shelling. They say you can get used to explosions.

I was very impressed by one scene in the city. Young trees had been planted next to the ruined, empty, windowless buildings of an old industrial plant, and there was a beautiful square with new benches, a playground, and a fountain. Such are the contrasts between the background of old Soviet infrastructure with the new landscape designs for public spaces. Life next to death next. In public spaces. The death of the age of the old empire, next to new life, new trees, freedom. There were many such images in the city. Such an energy for life in public spaces! And I thought that when leaves and flowers appeared on these saplings, when birds perched in their leaves, these contrasts would be even more pronounced. When I asked Tetiana how many kilometers it was to the demarcation line, she said she didn't know. Maybe 30, maybe 40. She's calmer not knowing for sure. Tetiana has already lost her house in Luhansk once, and may lose it again. We may all lose homes again, in a generation.

The Choir Of Death Of Russian Imperial Structures:

Instructions on how to surrender:
Forget your name
Discard the letters ï, €, r (yee as in yeast, ye as in yellow, huh as in hood)
Because they are not in the Russian alphabet.

If not, there will come a nuclear cloud
Beautiful as a Russian ballerina —
We will admire her flourish,
We will choke on her.
We will become familiar with the Gulag, repression
Forced deportations,
Executions of intellectuals
On the street of Friendship of Peoples,
With what green men from Crimea did not do.
Not aliens and enemies of the people
Not just our dictators
We've been masturbating over for generations,
We, all of us — will obey orders.
This is not Russophobia.
Absolutely not — we do what we need to,
What you do with yourself.
We will be tried in the Mariupol theater
Under the whistle of the post-industrial wind,
Maybe after death,
Maybe posthumously.

Voice Of A Plant That Doesn't Want To Be Uprooted From The Earth:

Then it began raining and snowing. There was a play and my premiere that I didn't even have time to think about. Maybe it doesn't matter anymore. At the moment, it is important to save people, help people, distribute and study instructions on how to act when there are shelling, chemical attacks, and rape. When you hear missiles, lie down, close your ears, and open your mouth. This will help reduce injury. This is the only thing I remember from the endless instructions that everyone sends to each other on social media horror.

Amid the instructions and the news, I came across a post from an acquaintance from Sievierodonetsk on Facebook. He published memoirs of how he joined the tree planting in the city two years ago – the same trees in the park that I had seen and imagined turning green.

Amid the instructions and news, I also came across a Facebook post from the head of the Luhansk district state administration, Serhiy Haidai, in which he published photos of fresh graves with wooden crosses from Irpin and Sievierodonetsk. He wrote: "There is a new cemetery in our district town. During the 52 days of the war, there have been more than 400 new graves. Currently, the city has about 20,000 inhabitants; on February 24th there were 130,000." The cemetery and wooden crosses resembled young leafless trees. I once saw such a cemetery in the middle of the city in Sarajevo. There are many old windowless ruins in this city too. There is also a river. Not so long ago, not so far. The Europe we wanted so much to go to. Ukraine will not go anywhere, you will always have time to travel there.

Trees are blooming. Cherries, apricots, apple trees. Magnolias are blooming and for the first time in my life I can't enjoy flowering. My time has stopped. Trees are blooming in Sievierodonetsk. Trees are blooming in Mariupol. They bloom in Kharkiv, in Sumy, and in Bucha . . . In occupied Vovchansk, where the man I love comes from — trees bloom.

Next year I would like to give my dad a tree for his birthday. Trees can unite demarcation lines with their roots, bind the burnt, mutilated Ukrainian land. Maybe I should buy a small potted tree. With instructions: The tree should be placed in a hole in the ground with plenty of space for the roots. The roots should not be folded or broken. The roots cannot be less than 20 centimeters long. Let this record stay here. May life always win.

Writing this text, I realized that I have a new dream — to go to the Donets and look at the water lilies at Saltiv, instead of going to Prague, to Chuhuiv not Oslo, through ruined Izium not California, to Rubizhne not Barcelona, to Lysychansk not Nancy, and to Sievierodonetsk and Luhansk and Donetsk, not Berlin. Even if there are no more cities, only water lilies. I dream of sailing along my favorite river in the east. I dream of experiencing the joy of flowers again. During the trip, I will snip a piece of water lily rhizome, dry it, and put it in my pocket. This flower, like the reflection of the sun, like the reflection of the heart, will protect me wherever I go. Strange dreams come in times of war.

JFa

Commissioned by a grant from Philip Arnoult's Center for International Theatre Development

THE RUSSIAN SOLDIER
IHOR BILYTS

[*Kitchen. Night. Pregnant Wife enters kitchen, does not turn on light. Russian Soldier sits at table.*]

WIFE. Fuck. Is that you?

RUSSIAN SOLDIER. Who else would it fucking be?

WIFE. What are you doing?

RUSSIAN SOLDIER. What do you fucking think? Don't turn on the light — I'm not here.

WIFE. Is that so? And where are you?

RUSSIAN SOLDIER. I'm lying near Chernihiv, fuck it. God-fucking-damn it.

WIFE. What the fuck am I supposed do? I'm having a fucking baby soon.

RUSSIAN SOLDIER. Don't ask me, I'm fucking not here. I don't fucking know what to do.

WIFE. So why did you come?

RUSSIAN SOLDIER. Fuck if I know, maybe say goodbye.

WIFE. Something to eat? Drink?

RUSSIAN SOLDIER. The fuck am I gonna drink? I'm not here.

WIFE. Oh.

RUSSIAN SOLDIER. Just don't cry.

[*Wife cries.*]

WIFE. Oh, fuck it.

[*Wife cries.*]

RUSSIAN SOLDIER. Don't cry — I'll fucking hit you.

WIFE. I won't.

[*Wife stops crying.*]

RUSSIAN SOLDIER. What's happ'nin' out there?

WIFE. No sugar.

RUSSIAN SOLDIER. That's fucked.

WIFE. So the fascist Banderites got you?

RUSSIAN SOLDIER. Who the fuck else?

WIFE. Bastards. What did they look like? Tell me.

RUSSIAN SOLDIER. I'm in a tank. What do I see?

WIFE. How will we know when they will come for us? How do we recognize them?

RUSSIAN SOLDIER. I'd like to see 'em myself. But I'm not here.

WIFE. If you're not, you're not. Quit fucking repeating it. If you're not, you're not.

[*Silence.*]

SON. Dad, is that you?

WIFE. Get the fuck out of here. Your dad's not here.

RUSSIAN SOLDIER. Don't say that, it's a forbidden word combination. Did you do your homework?

WIFE. He's in kindergarten.

RUSSIAN SOLDIER. Oh, fuck, forgot. Go to bed. Or I'll get out my belt.

SON. Are you at war, Dad?

RUSSIAN SOLDIER. What the fuck are you talking about?

WIFE. I'll put you in the corner. You can't say things like that.

RUSSIAN SOLDIER. You did a fucking hell of a job raising your son.

WIFE. So, where were you, asshole?

RUSSIAN SOLDIER. Defending the homeland, ever hear of that?

[*Silence.*]

RUSSIAN SOLDIER. Shame I can't drink. At least we celebrated Soldier's Day on February 23. Thanks for small favors.

WIFE. I can drink.

RUSSIAN SOLDIER. You're gonna have a baby.

WIFE. It doesn't fucking care.

RUSSIAN SOLDIER. My mother drank, too. Nothing good came of it. How's Dad?

[*Wife drinks.*]

WIFE. The bastard won't die, but now that's a plus — we'll live on his pension. Will they pay me for you?

RUSSIAN SOLDIER. They should. Ask at the base.

[*Wife drinks a second time. Doorbell rings.*]

WIFE. Who's that in the middle of the night?

RUSSIAN SOLDIER. Probably came for me. Just don't turn on the light.

[*Wife opens the door.*]

FSB AGENT. Is he here already?

WIFE. Sitting in the kitchen. He's not drinking.

FSB AGENT. You realize he's not there.

WIFE. I do. What of it?

FSB AGENT. What do you fucking think? Sign here.

WIFE. I'm not signing anything. I'll sign when I get my compensation.

RUSSIAN SOLDIER. Don't talk back at him — he'll throw you in prison.

FSB AGENT. You don't exist. You're not here. What compensation?

WIFE. I have a small child. I support my grandfather. I'm having a baby soon.

FSB AGENT. You, you still don't exist.

WIFE. What about me?

FSB AGENT. You're nobody.

[*There's no one here.*]

JFr

Commissioned by a grant from Philip Arnoult's Center
for International Theatre Development

THREE RENDEZVOUS
NATALKA VOROZHBYT

Rendezvous 1

[*A dark room. The laptop screen illuminates Maryna. She slips off her jeans, remains in her sweater. We don't see the screen — we just hear a man's voice from somewhere in the distance.*]

HE. Take it off already . . .

[*Maryna takes off her sweater and her T-shirt. She is cold, tries to wrap herself in a blanket, while leaving her intimate places in plain sight.*]

SHE. It's cold . . .

HE. Imagine me hugging you . . .

[*The door of the room is kept shut by a chair. Someone pulls on it from time to time, trying to open it. From the other side we hear,* "Mom, open up." "Maryna, should I defrost the fish?" "Where's the clay?" *etc.*]

HE. What's going on there?

SHE. It's in the room next door. Don't be distracted . . .

[*The dialogue between the lovers is precisely appropriate for the situation — phrases such as "show me," "lick," "do you for you," "Look, it's hard," "Don't stop," etc. She moans. He moans.*]

[*Gunshots and explosions are heard somewhere in the distance.*]

MARYNA. What is going on there?

HE. It's far away. Don't be distracted . . .

[*They try not to be distracted. She may be faking it.*]

• • •

[*The next room looks like a shelter. In it there are six beds and four women. Instead of nightstands — suitcases covered with things. A baby sleeps in a stroller. The women are mostly old. First Woman eats something. Second Woman is picking through medicines, rustling wads of plastic wrap. Third Woman sleeps, even snores. Fourth Woman reads the news on her smartphone, reads the reports loudly.*]

FOURTH. The Russian military began drawing up lists of local residents in occupied Kherson for the issuance of ten thousand rubles in order later to hold a referendum based on these lists . . .

SECOND. [*Hoarse voice, with hatred*] Damn it!! Damn them!

FIRST. Ten thousand is how much in grivens?

SECOND. What do you care about grivens, figure it in euros . . .

[*Fourth's smartphone jingles. She reads again.*]

FOURTH. Air raid alert. Head for cover immediately.

[*Third wakes up abruptly, gets up and immediately goes somewhere, clutching her purse to her breast. Everyone watches her go with surprise.*]

FOURTH. That's in Kharkiv. We're in Vienna.

[*Third looks at them angrily and leaves the room. Second twirls a finger at her temple.*]

[*Child runs into the room, goes to the closed door to the next room, and pulls on it repeatedly.*]

SECOND. Stay out of there. She's with your dad.

[*But Child does not stop pulling on the door.*]

CHILD. Mom! Where's Mom? Mom, open up!

[*Fifth Woman enters from the kitchen with a knife in her hands.*]

FIFTH. [*From the doorway*] Maryna, just tell me one thing — should I defrost the fish or boil sausages?

...

[*The room is dark. We hear the moans of a man and woman, we hear doors being pulled, and we hear gunshots and explosions through the laptop.*]

[*Maryna masturbates. She's already almost there. She is about to come.*

Accordingly, the dialogue between them is "Wait-wait, here it is . . . Oh, God . . . Oh, my God . . . so fucking good . . ." *Finally, she comes.*]

[*Somewhere in the laptop, a moan is interrupted by a particularly strong explosion, a scream, a blow. Silence. Maryna comes to her senses. She addresses the man somewhere in her laptop.*]

MARYNA. Yura, I'm done . . . Are you okay? Are you all right?! Where are you?! Can you hear me, Yura?! Yura?!!

[*The laptop screen is covered in blood. Maryna slaps her laptop shut like a coffin lid, covers her face with her hands, and sits there naked.*]

• • •

[*In a Viennese ski storeroom, Third Woman sits and listens to the peaceful but chaotic sounds of sirens, cars, the slam of doors, the screams of a child. Everything sounds new to her, and she trembles with fear.*]

Rendevous 2

[*Kyiv, spring, a square. Two men drink coffee — Pasha and Andriusha.* They are a little embarrassed and look closely at each other. A large pink suitcase on wheels stands next to Pasha.*]

---

*Since February 24, 2022, men aged 19 to 61 years are not allowed to leave Ukraine under wartime regulations.

ANDRIUSHA. So I went to the military enlistment office and I said, *"Take me. I'm ready."* They looked at me and said, *"Who are you?"* I said, *"I'm a cultural manager."* *"Who?!"* They laughed. *"How about uncultured, got any of them? It's the uncultured ones we need."* That's the level of their humor, in short. I say, I organize concerts, all sorts of events, I book festivals . . . They laughed again and said, *"Wait."* And I'm still waiting . . . Two months. I really am ready. Just give me a weapon.

PASHA. I have asthma. Problem is I'm unfit. I'd go. But I have a certificate.

ANDRIUSHA. Would you care to have another coffee?

PASHA. Why so formal?

ANDRIUSHA. [*Happily*] Okay. [*To the young waiter*] We'll have two more coffees. There used to be a really pretty waitress working here. Olia, right?

WAITER. She left. In Paris now.

[*The waiter accidentally bumps Pasha's suitcase. It falls over.*]

WAITER. Oh, sorry. I'm new here . . . [*Picks it up.*]

PASHA. [*Excuses himself*] They gave it to me at the shelter. Humanitarian aid.

ANDRIUSHA. What is she doing in Paris? What are they all doing there?

WAITER. They're all staying safe.

[*Andriusha takes out a pill and swallows it.*]

ANDRIUSHA. My gastritis has gotten worse. It's nerves.

PASHA. You shouldn't drink coffee.

ANDRIUSHA. What difference does it make? People are dying out there . . .

PASHA. It's hard for me to breathe here. I'm suffocating . . . It was easy to breathe in Mariupol . . .

ANDRIUSHA. Well, the breathing is better here now, Pasha . . .

PASHA. Yeah, yeah . . .

[*They drink coffee in silence for a while. Andriusha receives an alert signal on his phone. He watches a long time then grunts angrily.*]

PASHA. Listen. I want to ask you. You're the cultural manager . . . I'm a simple guy. A mechanic.

ANDRIUSHA. Ask away, Pasha.

PASHA. Are you sure you're not, you know? Because I exchanged text messages with this guy, and then we met. He seemed okay. We come to his place, and he has a double bed . . .

ANDRIUSHA. What do you mean?

PASHA. Well, I mean . . . He says, stay here. I say, fuck you. And went back to the shelter. Now they're fucking with me over there. I asked for a normal suitcase, and they gave me this thing.

[*Andriusha finally gets it.*]

ANDRIUSHA. Me?! What the hell? I'm not gay! I have a wife in Munich. You've got nerve!

PASHA. Well, all kinds of things can happen.

ANDRIUSHA. Look, I have two rooms. Sveta and I are in one room. The second is the kids' room. You can sleep in the nursery.

PASHA. When do they come back?

ANDRIUSHA. I don't know. Maybe never. They say it's quiet there. They're calm there. She always wanted to go there. Europe – shops, comfort, security. And I tell her – I want you to know I can't live there. I can only live in Ukraine, and that's that.

PASHA. Even if I could, they wouldn't let me out anyway.

ANDRIUSHA. I don't want to! I say, come home, it's quiet here. Then she reads the news in the morning and shouts at me that I'm a jerk and think only of myself.

[*An air raid alarm howls. The men look around. Waiter brings two more coffees. They drink silently. Andriusha has no desire to drink.*]

ANDRIUSHA. Are you sure you can cook? I can't do this anymore.

PASHA. I can also do borscht and cutlets.

ANDRIUSHA. And mashed potatoes with baked fish?

PASHA. Yes, I can. What's to do?

ANDRIUSHA. I'll clean up. I also know where they sell booze.

PASHA. [*Upset*] I'm a little low on cash . . .

ANDRIUSHA. Don't sweat it!

[*Shows a message on his phone.*]

ANDRIUSHA. See? She put 200 euros on my card. Svetka did. She says, "Eat well."

PASHA. She's worried.

ANDRIUSHA. Fuck that! I'll drink that money up, okay?

PASHA. You can't, you've got stomach problems.

ANDRIUSHA. She always says that, too . . .

PASHA. She loves you.

ANDRIUSHA. Uh-huh. There's a classmate there with her. Shit. Her first love. In Munich.

PASHA. Don't worry. When it's over, she'll come back. Nobody needs them there!

ANDRIUSHA. She's not coming back . . . They left us, Pasha. Get it through your head, they just up and left us!

[*Andriusha turns away. His shoulders tremble. Pasha gently puts his arm around his shoulders.*]

PASHA. It's good I got divorced before the war, and I don't give a flying fuck that she's hanging out somewhere in Warsaw. I don't give a damn, I can handle it . . . Calm down, Andriusha! [*Agitated; it is not clear who calms whom.*] Calm down! Let's go to the grocery store, curfew is coming soon. You wanted fish . . . We'll make some mashed potatoes.

[*They get up and walk towards the grocery store. Pasha rolls his pink suitcase across the cobblestones.*]

Rendezvous 3

[*Viennese embankment. Man, pleasant-looking, about 50, admires beautiful Woman and her 8-year-old Daughter. Woman teaches the child to skate but doesn't really know how to do it herself. They laugh, fall, stand up again, Daughter tries, the woman demonstrates how . . . Woman catches Man's eye, he smiles at her, she smiles politely back. Finally, the girl manages to get up on her skates, and she skates off.*]

[*The girl skates, the wind in her face. She is happy. Suddenly, something goes wrong. Woman screams and runs after her. Passers-by make way.*]

WOMAN. Turn left, Sonya, turn left! Slow down!

[*Man rushes forward and catches the girl, preventing her from falling. As Woman runs towards them, he holds the girl tight, strokes her, and says something soothing. Woman runs up, out of breath, and snatches her daughter out of his hands. Holds her tightly.*]

MAN. [*In German*] It's okay, she didn't fall . . .

WOMAN. [*Ungrateful*] Danke schön.

[*Woman abruptly takes Daughter and her skates, steps aside and says something to the child, looking at Man, as if giving him a warning. Man is puzzled by her reaction but smiles his usual smile.*]

• • •

[*The next morning. Man sits in a Viennese coffee shop, reads a newspaper. Suddenly sees Woman. She enters the cafe. She wears a long cloak. They check her vaccination certificate. Woman orders coffee to go, doesn't notice the man. Man watches her with interest. The bartender is in no hurry. Woman looks at her watch anxiously. Without waiting for her coffee, Woman leaves the coffee shop. Man picks up her coffee, pays for it, and tries to catch up with her.*]

• • •

[*Man follows her with the coffee. She doesn't notice him because she's using her GPS. He suddenly becomes interested in following her.*]

[*Woman arrives at Schwarzenbergplatz. Looks around. Locates the monument to a Soviet soldier.*]

[*Woman approaches the monument. Takes off her cloak, under which there is only a T-shirt. Woman is naked from the waist down. There is blood between her legs. Woman stands before the soldier.*]

[*Suddenly, she is joined by more women, all naked below the waist, all with bloodstained crotches. They stand and look at the Russian soldier. Passers-by are shocked. Someone takes pictures, someone passes by quickly. Man looks at Woman in shock. He sets down the coffee, turns, and leaves quickly.*]

JFr & NB

Commissioned by a grant from Philip Arnoult's Center
for International Theatre Development

EIGHT SONGS

YEVHEN MARKOVSKIY

[*Translator's note: I received these eight short songs about life under Russian occupation in the city of Kherson first as written texts, then, shortly thereafter, as audio recordings. They are performed in the style of traditional Tuvan throat singing which originated in Central Asia and/or China perhaps as early as 200 BCE. There is no link between traditional Ukrainian culture and that of Tuvan throat singing. Markovskiy's foray into the genre is a pastiche, but a brilliant one that plays wickedly with deadbeat nonchalance, tragedy and humor. I prepared the texts below keeping in mind at all times that these were not intended to be poems, but rather as lyrics to be sung and heard. I occasionally approximate the author's distinctive vocals, inserting references to the guttural sounds that he sings before, in between, and after some (but not all) lines of lyrics. These references are not intended as exact replications of what the performer sings, but to signal sonic shifts and give an approximation on paper of the way the songs unfold when sung. All that said, it seems to me that, even on the printed page, these lyrics reveal subtle and intriguing aspects of a life under enemy occupation that could be mundane, funny, harrowing, or all of those at the same time.*]

1. No Internet

I sit here with no internet,

I sit here with no internet,

I lie here with no internet.

Miau-miau-mia

Eee-rrrr-ooo-aah...

I sit here with no internet,

I sit here with no internet.

Aiy-ya-i-ya-I...

2. Everything Is Dead

You think everything here is dead?

That's not true, that's not true.

Marr-rrrarar-a-l...

This is Shumenskiy neighborhood.

The Shumenskiy micro-neighborhood.

3. Throat Singing

Rai-eeya-i-eeya-i-ee...

Throat singing as it's done in Kherson.

Oya-oia-aiya-aiya-uwa-uwa...

The Dnipro sleeps, the Dnipro seethes.

The Dnipro sings.

Oa-oa-oa-oh...

4. I'll Go Have a Bite

I'll go have a bite,

I'll go have a bite.

Of whatever was sent by Him who watches us all.

Aii-ya-i-aaiii-ya-i

Rrrr-ya-i-ya-i-yai . . .

I'll have a bite.

5. Freedom Square

I went downtown, I went downtown.

I wanted to grab a glimpse of life.

On every corner,

On every corner

A guy with a machine gun stands.

Oh-oh-oh!

Freedom Square,

Freedom Square,

Freedom Square,

Freedom Square.

Eee-ya-i-eee-ya-i-eee . . .

6. Slovianochka-Kubanochka

Everybody knows early of a morning,

At lunch or even before breakfast

Slovianochka tastes so good.

In everyone's house —

In Odesa and Lviv —

Slovianochka tastes so good.

In every house in every town

Slovianochka tastes so good.

Ukraine — the land of milk and honey,

Slovianochka tastes so good.

Slovianochka tastes so good.

Slovianochka tastes so g . . .

Slovianochka tastes so . . .

Slovianochka . . .

Slov . . .

Kubanochka is so tasty,

Kubanochka is so tasty,

Kubanochka is so tasty.

7. Kardymovo-Morgaushi

Ughghghghghgh . . .

Here comes the train,

Here comes the train

From Kherson

To Smolensk.

To Smolensk.

To Smolensk.

Aya-aya-eee . . .

Beer from Kardymov,

Eggs from Morgaushi.

Beer from Kardymov,

Eggs from Morgaushi.

Eeee-eeeyee-eee.

8. Marengo

I drank some Marengo.

I drank some Marengo.

All Shumenskiy is exploding.

I drank some Marengo.

I drank some Marengo.

There's nothing else I want so much.

I drank some Marengo.

I drank some Marengo.

Now I just want

To snore.

Rrrr-amm-dam-ya-i-eeee . . .

Yevhen Markovskiy reveals some details behind the images in the songs.

Songs 2. and 8.

The Shumenskiy district is a section of Kherson where almost a third of the city's population lived before the war. It is a so-called "bedroom community" located quite far from the city center. My family and I have lived in this area since 1977 when we received a three-room apartment. Of course, many memories and circumstances are associated with this place. Many friends and acquaintances, relatives, neighbors, and so on have lived there. This area was completely autonomous. There was no need to go into the city center for any reason. We had our own grocery stores, small shops, pharmacies, markets, a clinic, and veterinary services. It had everything a person needed to enjoy city life without ever having to leave the general area.

Song 6.

"Slovianochka" is a Ukrainian brand known for its canned goods, mayonnaise, produce in jars, dairy products and other such things.

"Kubanochka" is a Russian equivalent: the same basic thing, but Russian-made.

In the beginning I sing the song about "Slovianochka" in Ukrainian. It is an actual advertising jingle that you could hear in Kherson supermarkets up until March 2022.

In the end I switch to Russian and imitate – that is, parody – that same song, only this time singing about "Kubanochka," because after March 1, 2022, "Slovianochka" began disappearing from store shelves in Kherson, replaced by "Kubanochka."

As such, this song ironically symbolizes the change of reality in Kherson, wherein the Ukrainian city became Russian.

For obvious reasons there was a shortage of many goods and services in Kherson in March 2022. People had to stand in line in the cold for three to four hours just to buy a kilogram (two pounds) of potatoes. Even then, it was far from guaranteed that you would even get anything)))). I myself stood in such lines for many hours. I once managed to buy two rotten cabbages, but, as a result of the crush of people in the line, one of my shoes was shredded. That was very sad, because no other shoes were to be had at that time☺.

Song 7.

Meanwhile, Ukrainian beer, which everyone used to love and buy, also disappeared from stores in March. By around the middle of March, Russian beer began to be imported from Crimea. One of the imported brands was called Kardymovo beer. Kardymovo is a village in the Smolensk region of the Russian Federation where a brewery operates.

A similar story can be told about chicken eggs. In early March, they disappeared in Kherson. It was impossible to buy them. Before long, however, merchants appeared in open-air markets, or simply on the streets, who were selling "Morgaushi eggs," that is, eggs from the city of Morgaushi in the Republic of Chuvashia of the Russian Federation. By the way, they really were delicious!

The Kherson-Smolensk train mentioned in the lyrics is merely an allegory for events, nothing more. Obviously, no such route ever existed.

JFr

THREE ATTEMPTS TO IMPROVE DAILY LIFE
MAKSYM KUROCHKIN

The Stove

Because of the cold, dark sky, the expanses of the Kyiv Polissia — that endless span of forest — resemble northern climes. The stove in the big room is broken, and so as not to go brain-dead from carbon monoxide poisoning, we go outside to hang around.

I'm going to see the neighbor-woman Tonia for some clay. I bring Birov along for support.

Tonia explains convincingly that the soil in the village is too sandy. We'll have to go to the neighboring village. Then she smiles at her own bit of folly and pulls out a plastic bucket of fine, viscous clay.

I tell Birov we only got the clay because of his mustache. He doesn't object, but he doesn't acknowledge the topic either. He clings to his own thoughts. Birov is the Ukrainian form of the Hungarian "Biro," which means "judge." We've been together since day one. He is a friendly, conspicuous, loud kind of guy from western Ukraine. He never gets especially close to anyone, cares carefully for his body, and practices yoga. He throws himself 100 percent into everything he does. Sometimes I want to say: "Bro, don't worry over things so much. It's all a delusion, an illusion of relevancy." Of course, I say nothing.

I add sand and water as Tonia instructed me to do, and I knead the concoction. It can stand until morning.

Our battalion is stationed near Chernobyl in a village the Russians failed to reach because of the lack of normal roads. Actually, there is a road, but even we search for it for several hours, constantly bogging down in the sand. When we get stuck for good, two massive enchantresses emerge drunk from the furthest house down the line. They watch us as our driver struggles with his bare hands to untangle a cable wound round the front axle of the van. It's cold, I'm shivering, and the women offer advice. Finally having seen enough, the elder of the enchantresses brings us a crowbar.

By morning the next day, we have already managed to settle into two abandoned houses, and to clean up a third.

We carry out bags of rotted grain, swathes of glass wool, discolored leftover food, sweaty sweaters, numerous cans of expired canned goods, and dusty, dried-up mice. We put up family photos on a shelf. The village head says the owner will not return. He took a job with the prosecutor's office in a neighboring country, the bastard.

Our medic lights a fire, instantly chasing everyone out into the street. Smoke billows through holes in the chimney. Don't even dream of getting warm.

I ask who has experience repairing stoves. Nobody answers. That's a sign. I go to our neighbor for clay. I bring Birov along with me.

Then, as Tonia instructed, I add sand and water, and knead it. It's dark now. I'll start building the stove tomorrow. I have a notebook and two paperback books with me, but the IKEA heat candle doesn't provide much light. I prop up a regular candle from my volunteer's pack in a mug filled with fresh grain. I can read now. I'm asleep in five minutes.

In the morning, the voices in my head begin overwhelming me: All kinds of circumstances can interfere in the career of a stove builder. I prepare for the potential disputations with all my doubters.

The skeptics all froze during the night, and the stove is my responsibility. The foundation slid to the side, the chimney snapped, and you can put your fist through the cracks. I fill the crevices with broken bricks, but, still, I quickly run out of clay.

The voices of my thoughts grow louder. They won't let me think. I need to find the village head again. Fortunately for me, he's drinking coffee outside, watching the Kostenki brothers build a modernist toilet. Limping, the local community leader leads me to a vacant lot and there, among the heaps of houses, he shows me how to extract clay from beneath the remains of other collapsed chimneys.

I've filled in the cracks, but my access to raw materials has awakened new ambitions. If you look closely, you'll find bricks that can be freed from their smooth, whiteish mortar. I suspect that's how they cleaned the flues. I try breaking the bricks off with a knife, and it turns out not to be so difficult. Two hours later, I'm dirty as hell, but almost happy. With each tub of soot I remove, the people of my inner voices gradually quiet down.

Our cook Benia was the first to find out about it. No one believed him.

The next morning, I lit the stove, confirmed that all the smoke was rising into the chimney, and managed to warm my hands.

Then we loaded our ordnance into the shishiga, our GAZ-66 transport truck, got in our vans, and headed for a new location.

The Trench

Birov tells me how he toured America with Hare Krishnas. I respond by telling him about New York, sandwiches purchased on Houston Street, and the grilled ribs that Mexicans make in Austin, Texas. It's almost mid-May, but the wind in Luhansk is cold, and it cuts like steel. Birov and I dig a trench. We're frightened to spend another night in the open air. The earth is gooey, and we dig down slowly. We hide beneath the trees when a drone flies overhead.

As we were decamping to our positions two days ago, we misplaced a sapper shovel that we had brought all the way from Kyiv. Now it has come back to me, even if it is quite blunted. I am in great spirits. The universe is under control again. We have incurred no injuries. We are fortunate. We are not pencils — we are kings.

We call our position "Customs." We are on high ground, although sometimes I think we are at the lowest point of Earth's giant basin. Above us is the forest, whence come drones and mines. Above us is a valley where multiple rocket launch systems do their work. There is also one of those waste dumps, a terrikon, and a distant mineshaft. We have been manning roadblocks for so long, waiting for real work, that now we don't perceive reality with full adequacy: Explosions for us are like movies we expect to see. We are pencils, barely trained members of the territorial defense. We are not merely surrounded. We are not merely at ground zero. We are present where the Ukrainian army has not set foot in years. We walk around our position standing tall, lively, and cheerful, although this territory on our maps is marked in the colors of the enemy.

Our esteemed Troian has returned from the village with a backpack full of food and water. Things are looking up. Someone is even brewing coffee on the gas burner.

Birov plans to write a novel and make films. He is full of ideas and observations about life. I finally have a friend I can hang out with all night long. He's funny and frank.

I mark the outlines of a future foxhole in the ground. It will be the best foxhole in the world. Over the stove I will affix a magnet of the folk hero Cossack Mamai which I have carried with me from the first day. The foxhole will be cozy and cheerful. I dig and dig and dig. I even get a little overheated, so I remove my fleece jacket and hide it under a bush. Oh, how I will regret that in the coming days.

They started pounding us around noon. They pounded us right out.

Christina's World

I am asleep, but my eyes are open. I peer into the woods on the other side of a small clearing. Three days have passed, but it will take the rest of my life to tell about them without resorting to lies.

I see Birov wherever I look. We keep talking, even though he's been killed.

They drove us out not only from our bad position, but from the center of the village, too. We are waiting for a new offensive. We have not been rotated out.

An hour ago, I contrived a way to reconcile myself with what is happening. I crouched down on the ground not as soldiers are taught to do, but rather the way the woman does in the famous painting by Andrew Wyeth. Except I keep my back straight and my hand rests on a Kalashnikov. This way I see everything in the world, not just in my sector. I'm ready for anything that might happen. The voices of the people in my head are finally silent.

I crouch under a tree, snapping off acacia twigs that I can reach with my free hand, and I plant them in the ground. It's judicious. It is camouflage. It increases my chances of being the first to shoot. This now is the height of my ambitions.

JFr & NB

BIOGRAPHIES

The 20 Writers of the Kyiv Theater of Playwrights (ToP)

PAVLO ARIE is a Ukrainian playwright, conceptual artist, and theater director. He was educated at universities in Ukraine and Germany. He has lived in Lviv, Cologne, and Kyiv. An exhibition of his art and installations was held in Bonn in 2016. He translated Sarah Kane's *Blasted* into Ukrainian. He worked with other Ukrainian playwrights at the Royal Court Theatre in London in 2011 and was the artistic director of the Lesia Ukrainka Drama Theater in Lviv in 2016. He is the author of more than a dozen plays written in Ukrainian, German, and Russian. His first play was *Ten Ways to Commit Suicide*, written in 2004. His plays have been published in four collections.

OLENA ASTASEVA was born in the city of Kherson, which she considers her hometown to this day, although she currently is in exile outside of Ukraine. She studied at the Kyiv Institute of Culture. She has worked as a librarian, a bookseller, and a copywriter, and she taught courses in playwriting in Kherson. She is the author of stories and a number of plays that were repeatedly shortlisted for the Ukrainian *Contemporary Play Week* festival and were staged in the theaters of Kherson and Kyiv. Her short play *A Dictionary of Emotions in a Time of War* has been presented, read, performed, and filmed in a dozen countries since it was written in March 2022.

IHOR BILYTS studied at the Karpenko-Kary National University of Theatre, Film, and Television in Kyiv. He worked as an actor in the Dyvniy Zamok Theatre-Studio in Kyiv and debuted as a playwright in September 2017 with *Gay Parade* at Ukrainian *Contemporary Play Week*. In January 2018, *Gay Parade* premiered at the Wild Theatre in Kyiv. His second play, *How to Steal a Horse,* opened in November 2018 with the support of Renaissance Foundation. His play *Prostitute* was chosen for the shortlist of *Drama.UA* in December 2018 and was staged at the Theater Neft in Kharkiv in 2019. In December 2021 his recent play, *Captive,* was shortlisted at *Drama.UA.*

NATALIA BLOK is a playwright and screenwriter. Her plays have been staged with success in Ukraine (at state and independent theaters) and abroad. Her texts have repeatedly been shortlisted for prestigious international and national competitions: Ukrainian *Contemporary Play Week, Batumi Monoplay Festival*, *Drama.UA, Coronation of the Word,* and *Pitching for State Cinema*. Her work has been translated into Polish, Georgian, German, English, and Russian. She is a multiple winner of the *Pitching for State Cinema* competition as a screenwriter.

ANDRIY BONDARENKO holds a doctor of philosophy degree and is a playwright, screenwriter, and culturologist. He has worked primarily as a journalist, in particular as a cultural observer. He was also a researcher at the Center for Urban History of Central and Eastern Europe (Lviv). He is currently the head of the literary and dramatic department (dramaturge) at the Lviv Puppet Theater. Plays by Bondarenko, such as *Interview with a Friend* (2019) and *Asshole* (2020) were produced in Ukraine, and have appeared in shortlists of such Ukrainian festivals as *Contemporary Play Week, Drama.UA,* and *The*

Festival of Drama of Love and Beaver, where they were presented in the format of readings. His play, *Clout* (2022), premiered at the Lviv Puppet Theater.

VITALIY CHENSKIY is a playwright, screenwriter, and novelist. He was born in Mariupol and educated at Azov Technical University. He worked at the Azovstal metallurgical plant for seven years. In 2005, he moved to Kyiv, worked as a journalist, and began writing prose and plays that were published in such journals as *Union of Writers*, *Modern Drama*, *Sociologie et Sociétés*, and others. He participated in such international projects as *Ukrainian Festival 2016* (Theater Magdeburg) and *Eine Brücke aus Papier 2018* ("Paper Bridge"). Performances based on his plays *Vitalik* and *Aeneid XXI* were winners of the *All-Ukrainian Theater Festival* GRA/GRA Award.

JULIA GONCHAR was born in Kyiv and splits her time between writing and a career in international project management. After completing her bachelor's and master's degrees in international business and management, she worked on various theater projects in the areas of dramaturgy and public relations. Since 2012 she has been part of the young drama activist scene in Ukraine. Productions of her plays have been staged in Georgia, Germany, Switzerland, Austria, and Thailand. In 2020 she became a co-founder of the Theater of Women Playwrights in Kyiv, which focuses on the texts of contemporary women authors.

OKSANA GRYTSENKO is a Ukrainian playwright and screenwriter. She wrote her first play, *Saniok*, in 2019 following completion of courses in dramatic writing conducted by Maksym Kurochkin and Anastasiia Kosodii. This play was shortlisted at the Ukrainian *Contemporary Play Week* in 2019 and had a staged reading at Lesia Ukrainka Drama Theater in Lviv. Her second play, *Don Juan from Zhashkiv*, was shortlisted at *Contemporary Play Week* in 2020. Based on this play, Grytsenko created a screenplay for a feature film with the same name. The film was produced by Kristi Films and was funded by Ukraine's State Film Agency. The release of the film was scheduled for December 2022. Before starting her artistic career, Grytsenko worked as a journalist for about 20 years, covering the Russian invasion of Georgia, Ukraine's EuroMaidan Revolution, Russia's annexation of Crimea, and Russia's war against Ukraine. She has worked for Ukrainian and foreign publications, including the *Kyiv Post, AFP, The Guardian, Pittsburgh Post-Gazette, Marie Claire, Ukraine Verstehen, Huck Magazine, Nikkei,* and the *Wall Street Journal*.

OLENA HAPIEIEVA was born in the city of Sumy and studied directing in Kharkiv and Moscow. As a director she has staged Natalka Vorozhbyt's *Demons* and other contemporary texts. Her own dramatic texts include *Apartment, Sisters, Passerby; Tell Me Only Good Things;* and *Dad.* These were shortlisted and presented as staged readings at the *Contemporary Play Week* festival. The war of the Russian Federation against Ukraine forced her and her two children, five years and one year, eight months, into exile beginning in Mykolaiv, continuing on to Odesa, Lviv, Poland, and from there to Rouen, France. She writes short texts based on her experience and considers her work a means to understanding reality.

IRYNA HARETS is a playwright, writer, screenwriter, director, and psychologist, and the head of the Theater of Modern Dialogue in Poltava. She has been a finalist and winner of Ukrainian and international drama and literary competitions, and she is an experienced trainer in such fields as civic competence, creating social theater venues, non-formal education for children and adults, and creative thinking. She is the author and curator of social projects and is the founder of the All-Ukrainian Library of Contemporary Drama (UkrDramaHub). She was a nominee for the Women in Arts 2021 Award, in the category "Women in Theater."

ANASTASIIA KOSODII is from Zaporizhzhia and Kyiv. She is a Ukrainian playwright and director. She was a co-founder of the New Drama Theater in Zaporizhzhia. Before the full-scale Russian invasion of 2022, Anastasiia often worked with NGOs in Eastern Ukraine in towns on the front line of the ongoing war (2014–2022) between Ukraine and Russia. Her international work has most often been connected with the Maxim Gorki Theater in Berlin and the Münchner Kammerspiele Theater. After the Russian invasion, Anastasiia temporarily moved to Germany. She organized a series of readings under the title of *Vom Krieg* (About the War — Ukrainian Playwrights Tell of Life During the Russian Invasion) in a number of theaters around the world, including the Royal Court Theatre (London), Münchner Kammerspiele, Gorki Theater (Berlin), NTM Nationaltheater Mannheim, Schauspielhaus Wien, Staatstheater Hannover, and ETA Hoffmann Theater (Bamberg). In the fall of 2022, Anastasiia will begin work as a writer-in-residence at National Theater Mannheim.

MAKSYM KUROCHKIN, a playwright and screenwriter, is one of the most respected writers in Ukraine. Born in Kyiv, he graduated from the Shevchenko National University where he studied history and archaeology. In the late 1990s, he graduated from the Gorky Institute of Literature in Moscow and split his time between Kyiv and Moscow for the next 18 years. One of his first staged plays was *Fighter Class Medea* in Vilnius, Lithuania, in 1996. His early iconic productions include *Kitchen* (Moscow, 2000), *Stalova Volya* (Kyiv, 2001), *Repress and Excite* (Moscow, 2008), *The Schooling of Bento Bonchev* (Moscow, 2010; Austin, Texas, 2012), *Dulcey and Roxy at City Hall* (Austin, Texas, 2014), *Vodka, Fucking, and Television* (Moscow, 2006; Austin, Texas, 2012; Kyiv, 2017), *Titus the Immaculate* (Moscow, 2016), and *Be Silent, Oedipus* (Moscow, 2016). He returned to live and work permanently in his native city of Kyiv in 2017. Some of his major works during this period were *Russiaphobia*, *Kherson*, *Asexuals*, *Laurels*, and *Tolik the Milkman* (a free riff on *Tevye the Milkman*). His plays have been translated into many languages and performed around the world. Kurochkin is the co-founder and artistic director of the Theater of Playwrights in Kyiv.

TETIANA KYTSENKO is a playwright and screenwriter. She specializes in social and psychological drama. She has won numerous awards at Ukrainian *Contemporary Play Week* (Kyiv, 2011, 2012, 2013), the *Drama.UA* festival (Lviv, 2012), and the *Coronation of the Word* competition (Kyiv, 2015). She has participated in the festival *SPECIFIC* (Brno, Czech Republic, 2014) and the Wilder Osten Ereignis Ukraine project (Magdeburg, Germany, 2016). She was awarded the Grand Prix of the Free Theater competition (London-Minsk, 2016), and was a curator of the following events: *To Document!; Drama Of Freedom; and Insight Contemporary Drama* (Kharkiv). She was author and curator of the socio-artistic *Vitally Important* project (2018–2019). She is a member of the Board of the Theater Platform NGO (Kyiv), and a member of the Supervisory Board of the Ukrainian League of Authors.

LENA LAGUSHONKOVA was born in the village of Stanitsa Luhanska in Ukraine, and she graduated from the history department of Taras Shevchenko National University in Luhansk. She debuted as a playwright in 2018 with the play *BAZA*, about women and prostitution. She is the playwright-in-residence at the Vasylko Theater in Odesa. Her short plays have been presented at numerous festivals, including Ukrainian *Contemporary Play Week*, *Drama.UA*, and *Aurora*.

OLHA MACIUPA is a Ukrainian playwright and theater critic. She holds a doctor of philosophy degree in humanities. Her plays have been shortlisted at the following drama competitions: *Contemporary Play Week*, *Drama.UA*, and *Transmission.UA: Drama on the Move* at the Ukrainian Institute. Maciupa's dramatic works have been produced in Ukraine and Poland, in particular in Lviv, Khust, Sievierodonetsk, Rzeszów, and Sosnowiec. Her most recent play, *Eco Ballad*, premiered in the Ukrainian city of Chernivtsi in May 2022.

YEVHEN MARKOVSKIY is an actor, director, and playwright who was born in Kherson. Since 2003 he has worked as a journalist for various print and electronic publications. He worked as a correspondent for the TV channels Inter, 1+1, and TRK Ukraine. He was one of the leaders of the Kherson Meyerhold Center and is the author of the plays *Kill the Giver*, *Cuntsuffering*, *The Party*, *Dovboyoba*, *Scanning*, *ichloM*, *Cursed Creatures*, *Flowers and Roots*, *I'll Put it in Good Hands*, and *Kachkonis*. He has been a resident at the Royal Court Theatre (London), and in theater programs in Berlin and Potsdam. His text, *The Party*, was translated into English, German, Polish, and Czech. *Scanning* and *Cuntsuffering* have been produced on stage.

KATERYNA PENKOVA was born in Donetsk. She graduated as a spoken-word actor from the Kyiv State Academy of Popular and Circus Arts. Her plays have been shortlisted at *Drama.UA*, *Contemporary Play Week,* and the *Lyubimovka* festival in Moscow. She was awarded first prize at the *Coronation of the Word* competition. She was one of the winners of the drama competition of the Ukrainian Institute in the framework of *Transmission.UA: Drama on the Move*, Germany (2020). Productions of her works include *I Don't Remember the Title*, Chernihiv Youth Theater; and *A Family History*, co-authored with Lena Lagushonkova, at the Afanasiev State Academic Puppet Theater in Kharkiv.

OKSANA SAVCHENKO was born and raised in Kyiv. She is a screenwriter, playwright, and journalist. As a screenwriter, she has worked with television channels TRK Ukraine, Inter, and with the FILM.UA media company. As a playwright she participated at the *Heidelberger Stückemarkt Theater Festival* (2017) in Germany, the international *Telpa Daugavpils* festival in Latvia (2014), and *Contemporary Play Week* in Kyiv. She has collaborated with Georg Genoux and Natalka Vorozhbyt's Theater of Displaced People. In 2011, she participated in the London Royal Court theatre program for Ukrainian playwrights.

LIUDMYLA TYMOSHENKO was born in Kazakhstan and graduated in 2000 from the Faculty of Philosophy of Ivan Franko National University of Lviv. She is a candidate for a degree in philosophical sciences, and she holds a doctor of philosophy degree in political sciences. She is a playwright, screenwriter, artist, and university lecturer. Her plays have been shortlisted annually for Ukrainian and foreign drama competitions and festivals. Two premieres were scheduled for February–May 2022 at theaters in Kyiv and Lviv, neither of which took place due to the Russian invasion of Ukraine.

NATALKA VOROZHBYT is a Ukrainian playwright and a leader in the resurgence of Ukrainian national drama in the 21st century. Her first major play, *Galka Motalko,* had success shortly after she graduated from Moscow's Gorky Literature Institute in 2000. *The Grain Store*, a historical work about the Holodomor, the state-induced famine in Ukraine in the 1930s, was produced by the Royal Shakespeare Company in London in 2009. Vorozhbyt took part in the Euromaidan protests in Kyiv in 2013–2014, and the theme of the ensuing war with Russia has colored her work ever since. In 2015, she was a co-founder, with Georg Genoux, of the Theatre of Displaced People, which offered an opportunity for refugees from the Donbas region to tell their stories in a formal, theatrical context. She wrote the screenplay for *Cyborgs*, a 2017 film about the bloody defense of an airport in Donetsk against Russian separatists. *Bad Roads* (2017) was staged at the Royal Court Theatre in London, and, as a film directed by the author, was Ukraine's official Oscar selection in 2022. Although she wrote in Russian early in her career, Vorozhbyt now writes in Ukrainian.

TRANSLATORS

JOHN FREEDMAN is an American writer and translator who, after working for 30 years in Russia, now resides in Greece. He lived in Moscow from 1988 to 2018, where he was the theater critic of *The Moscow Times* (1992–2015). His play *Dancing, Not Dead* (2011) was winner of the Internationalists Global Play Contest (2011) and his short play, *Five Funny Tales from the Heart of Buenos Aires* (2013), has been performed in New York City, Chattanooga, and Edinburgh. He has translated over 100 plays, of which productions have been mounted in five continents. He is the author or compiler of numerous books, including *Silence's Roar: The Life and Drama of Nikolai Erdman* (1992) and *Provoking Theater: Kama Ginkas Directs* (2003). He was Russian director of The New Russian Drama: Translation/Production/Conference (2007–2010) conducted by Towson University and the Center for International Theatre Development (CITD); and director of New American Plays for Russia (2010–2015), a CITD project bringing cutting edge American drama to Russia with the support of the U.S. embassy in Moscow under the auspices of the Bilateral Presidential Commission. He is the curator of two Worldwide Play Readings projects: *Insulted. Belarus* (2020 to present) and Ukrainian Play Readings (2022 to present). He is the director of CITD's Ukrainian Hope Initiative.

NATALIA BRATUS graduated in 1982 with a degree in metallurgical engineering in her hometown of Dnepropetrovsk (now Dnipro), Ukraine, the Soviet Union. She worked as a defectoscopist engineer for ten years before becoming a private entrepreneur after Ukraine declared independence. She escaped the war in Ukraine with her daughter, grandson, and two family pets in March 2022, and immediately began working with John Freedman on translations of Ukrainian dramatic texts.

JOHN FARNDON is a writer, poet, playwright, and songwriter living in London, and a translator of literature from Eurasia, including plays for the Worldwide Ukrainian Play Readings (2022). He has written over a thousand books on science, nature, and other topics, translated into most languages and shortlisted five times for the Young People's Science Book Prize. His translations of the poetry of Lidia Grigorieva were nominated for five major awards, including the Griffin. He was joint winner of the 2019 EBRD Literature Prize for translating the poetry in Uzbek writer Hamid Ismailov's *The Devil's Dance*, and a finalist for the 2020 US PEN translation award for his translation of Kazakh writer Rollan Seysenbaev's *The Dead Wander in the Desert*. His translations of the lyrics of Vladimir Vysotsky were published as *Vladimir Vysotsky, Selected Works* by Glagoslav Publications in 2022. He ran the Arc venue at the *Edinburgh Fringe Festival,* and the Cauldron series of poetry and music events. He was chair of the Eurasian Creative Guild 2019–2021.

EVGENIA KOVRYGA is a director and writer, originally from Ukraine. She graduated with a master of arts degree in advanced theatre practice at the Royal School of Speech and Drama in London in 2021.